MW01592409

A Memoir

A Memoir

It's All About Me

Emily Lourigan

Copyright © 2025 by Emily Lourigan.

ISBN: Softcover   979-8-3694-4587-7

All rights reserved. No part of this book may be reproduced or transmitted
in any form or by any means, electronic or mechanical, including photocopying,
recording, or by any information storage and retrieval system,
without permission in writing from the copyright owner.

This is a work of fiction. Names, characters, places and incidents either are the
product of the author's imagination or are used fictitiously, and any resemblance
to any actual persons, living or dead, events, or locales is entirely coincidental.

Any people depicted in stock imagery provided by Getty Images are models,
and such images are being used for illustrative purposes only.
Certain stock imagery © Getty Images.

Print information available on the last page.

Rev. date: 05/29/2025

To order additional copies of this book, contact:
Xlibris
844-714-8691
www.Xlibris.com
Orders@Xlibris.com
867205

CONTENTS

Dedicated to my daughter Michele
and my grandchildren Emily, Christopher, and Sarah

ACKNOWLEDGMENTS

Thank you to my late husband Les, Dr. Bob and Bill W.
for giving me the courage and tools to keep going.
Thank you to my granddaughters, Emily and Sarah Ruzicka
for filling in for my lack of computer knowledge.
Barbara Hamilton and Bob Herion for the final drafts.
Thank you to Frank Eighmey for helping with the history.
Gloria, Sharon, Donna for keeping me accountable.
And finally Mike Chappelle for the subtitle.
Finally, thank you to Betty Smith and Louisa May
Alcott for showing me the true joy of reading.

CHAPTER 1

A Thanksgiving Memory

This is the story of my first memory. Most of it is based on what holidays and special occasions looked like at my house as I was growing up. I suppose some of it is how I wished it had been, and some of it must have really happened the way I am going to tell it.

The dining room table had all the leaves in it, so it was as long as it could get. The red tablecloth was showing underneath the white crocheted tablecloth my mother had created. Most of the dishes that were usually on display in our white hutch were on the table or in the kitchen waiting to be filled with all the food my mom was cooking. A couple of mismatched salt and pepper shakers didn't make it to the table along with two or three small plates and a figurine of Santa Claus that would need to wait till Christmas to be displayed. Dinner plates, cups and saucers, silverware and napkins of assorted designs and styles were set ready for the meal to be served. A big platter with homemade bread and butter pickles, dill pickles, radishes cut like roses, celery sticks and green olives with pimentos was on a small side table.

The windows had been washed, the curtains were clean and the furniture was dusted. There was a chair in front of each place setting, one for each of us: my Dad, mother, sister Shirley, brother John and me. There was also one each for the cousins who were at all our celebrations: Fred, Bernice and their son Connie. Anita had left home and was working in Alaska. Allan was in the Navy stationed on the USS Quincy. Because we lived on Quincy Street, I don't know how old I was before I realized that all the sailors in the Navy were not on a ship that had the same name as the street they lived on.

The living room was separated from the dining room with a curtain rod that on most days had clothes hanging on wire hangers. There were not enough closets and when the ironing got done, that's where the clothes were put. But on this day, they were in the bedroom off the living room. Several chairs, a davenport, a couple of lamps, a hassock and a picture on the wall all filled the space of the little living room. That picture hung in the same place for probably twenty years; I must have looked at it every day, and I have no idea what the subject was. The furniture changed as often as my mom could afford a new second- or third-hand piece. The wallpaper never once was put up so the seams matched. Half a rose was on one strip, and halfway down the next strip was the other half of the rose.

The kitchen always looked the same, anchored by a small gas stove with the name Robert Shaw printed on the oven control. Four burners and a small oven produced wonderful pies, homemade bread and rolls, coffee cakes and cookies at Christmas, pecan pralines, divinity and fudge. Plum jam, grape jelly and rhubarb sauce were made from the trees and plants in our yard. I need to be honest here because I would never have admitted it when I was growing up. I don't ever remember the oven getting cleaned. Maybe it was–I just never cleaned it and never saw anyone else do it. The table was just big enough to hold all the pots, pans and jars needed for the canning and jelly making. The enamel was just a little more worn than that on the stove top. The icebox was tiny. The freezer held one ice cube tray, and defrosting it was a job put off until it wasn't possible to put even that in it. Defrosting called for setting hot water in a small dish on the shelf over and over again and then emptying the melted ice out of the pan under the tiny freezer compartment.

The kitchen sink was probably installed when the house was built. The enamel was chipped in a dozen places, and there were stains in it from so many plums and peach skins that it was no longer white. It was necessary to turn on the hot water heater thirty minutes before we washed the dishes. Above the sink a windowsill held a cracked tea cup, a small ball of rubber bands, a little glass cup used for washing out eyes, two or three little corn on the cob holders, a pen with the ink used up, two jacks and a cracked red ball to play with if we ever found the other eight jacks.

It was a fairly typical kitchen in an old house in Waterloo, Iowa. The unique addition was some sort of a pipe that had some plumbing function, although I never did find out what it was for. It was about eight inches wide and painted some combination of brown and green. It ran from the ceiling to the floor and was used as a storage area for every brown bag ever brought into the kitchen. Some women collected matching cups and saucers and souvenir plates. My mother collected buttons and brown paper bags. My brother-in-law Frank's favorite story is one of how much she hoarded them. She was going to send a loaf of homemade bread home with my sister's family, and Frank reached for one of the bags to put it in. Now there were probably at least a hundred of them, all different sizes. Ma yelled at him.

"Frank, what are you doing? You put that bread in this piece of newspaper. You know I'm saving those sacks in case I need them!" Paper bags are called sacks in the Midwest or at least that's what they were called in 1950.

Scene One

You know when you open a playbill and the scene has been described under the player's names and characters? My memory has just staged the setting and the cast.

The action begins: (All talking at once)

BERNICE. Freda, everything was so good and I think I want another spoonful of sweet potatoes.

SHIRLEY. Ma, tell John to stop chewing so loud. Ma, is Anita having dinner with Aunt Fern?

MA. I think so. At least she's with part of the family. I wonder how Allan is and what he is having to eat?

CONNIE. Aunt Freda, I'm glad you baked a mince pie. Did you remember they are my favorite?

DAD. Maybe later, John and I will take a walk up to the yards and see what freight trains are in.

JOHN. I can't today, Dad. Bob is coming to play catch later. Is that okay if I miss today?

FRED. I'll go with you, John. I need to get some fresh air.

Emily is quiet. She's just listening

All of a sudden during all this small talk, there is a banging on the back
    porch door. Everyone is again talking at once:
"What's going on? Who could that be? Whoever it is, why are they at the
    back door? No one ever uses that."
ALLAN. Where is everybody? Unlock the door!
MA. Oh my heavens, it's Allan!!!
Ma and Shirley are crying.
FRED. Freda, you just said Allan's name, and now he's here. SHIRLEY.
    I can't believe he's really here!
MA. When did you get here? How long can you stay?

I have no idea what's happening. I start to cry too. I'm scared because
it got so loud and I don't know who this tall man is that is coming into the
dining room. He's laughing and waving his white cap in the air while he
hugs my mother. He picks me up and swings me around, kisses me on the
cheek and sets me down again.

Shirley runs around the table, hugs me and says, "Don't cry. It's your
brother Allan. You know, we talk about him all the time but you don't
recognize him because you were just a little girl when you saw him last."

"Oh man, am I hungry. I've been on my way home since yesterday and
haven't had much to eat. I'm sure glad there is plenty of food left." "Shirley,
please get a plate and silverware, and Allan, sit down while we get some
food for you."

"I'll sit in a minute, but first I have to look at everybody. I can hardly
believe I'm really here."

It's very quiet now as he walks around the table and speaks to each one
of us in a private, hushed voice, not at all like it was just a few minutes ago.
He kneels down and puts his hand on my head. "What a pretty girl you are. I
bet you're really smart, too, aren't you? Did Shirley help you braid your hair?"

He stands up and puts his arm around Shirley as she walks by him
carrying dishes and a coffee cup. "You are so grown up. A lot of my Navy
buddies would be really jealous if they knew I had such a cute sister. When
I get back to the ship, I hope you will write me a letter and send a picture
so I can show you off."

He shakes hands with Fred and Connie and hugs Bernice and tells them
how nice it is they could be there to celebrate Thanksgiving with "the folks."

John looks like he's afraid Allan will hug him, too, but Allan shakes
his hand first and then cuffs him on the shoulder.

"Joe DiMaggio had a pretty good year, didn't he? Are you going to play baseball next year? I bet you're pretty good, right? I'm guessing you're a pitcher, right?"

He hugs my father and shakes his hand, too. "How are things at the yards? Do you get there every day? When was the last time you went to Chicago on *The Land O'Corn?*"

He sits down on the chair put there next to his dishes. He goes to my mother, brings her over, and sits her on his lap. She is still crying softly. "Ma, you look pretty good after cooking all morning. It's a good thing you made all my favorites, or I might have turned around and gone over to Mrs. Lown's for dinner. If I had done that though, I might have been too sick to go back to the ship. What do you think about that? It sure is good to see you." No one had said anything as he was asking his questions. It remained quiet until he picked up my mother, set her back in her chair and hollered, "LET'S EAT!"

This scene took place seventy–two years ago. If it actually took place the way I wrote it, I'm not certain. However, it is the way I remember it and wish it had been.

WEDNESDAY, NOVEMBER 13, 1968   Page Thirty-three

Traditional Ceremony for Navy

Navy Chief Boatswain's Mate Allan D. Engleman recited poetry to Hancock's crew a Keystone Kop as part of the entertainment during Shellback initiation ceremonies aboard the attack carrier USS Hancock. Engleman recited oetry to Hancock's crew during the ritualistic ceremonies when Han-cock crossed the equator recently en route to Singapore. He is the son of Mr. and Mrs. J. H. Engleman, of 227 Quincy St., and is Hancock's Chief Master-at-Arms. The Alameda, Calif.-based carrier, commanded by Capt. Howard E. Greer, is presently deployed on her fourth Vietnam cruise.

Allan, looking like a Keystone Cop   *John showing off at age 10*

CHAPTER 2

Two Stories About How I Figured Out Why Movies are Important

Movies have always played an important part in how I learned to live in the world. They showed me how to behave if I were ever to be invited to a dinner party. What a dinner party even was! I saw how people lived in other parts of the country. I saw rich people, poor people. I saw how to see the good guys and how to spot the bad guys. This wasn't always accurate, as I came to find out when I got older. I would never have been able to know what California or Paris or Germany was like if movies weren't part of my growing up. I learned about racism and fear and lying from movies like *To Kill a Mockingbird*. I thought love was supposed to be like Cary Grant and Deborah Kerr in *An Affair to Remember* and what it could look like in *Who's Afraid of Virginia Woolf*. I cried when Francie found the flowers on her desk at her graduation in *A Tree Grow in Brooklyn*. I was furious when Ashley Wilkes and Scarlett O'Hara were so wishy-washy in *Gone with the Wind*. I wanted to yell at the screen and tell them "Scarlett, stop being such a brat and Ashley, get a backbone!" Most of all, wasn't Melanie Wilkes such a sickeningly sweet Southern Belle?

There are family stories about *Barry Lyndon, Tender Mercies, The Godfather and West Side Story*.

One of my favorite family stories is about a person, not a movie. My sister Shirley and my mother told me about the time a cousin of theirs had gone with them to some unspecified show starring Fred Astaire and Ginger Rogers. They were looking at the poster of the movie, and our cousin was very confused. She wanted to know who the male dancer was in the picture. Shirley explained, "It's Fred Astaire." Our cousin sputtered, "That can't be right. Freda Staire is a woman." When they explained how she had made a mistake, it became family lore. My mother's name was Freda Engleman. The cousin had assumed the actor and my mother had the same first name, just pronounced differently. Therefore Freda Staire had to be a woman. (If I could insert an emoji here it would have to be a smiley face).

I live in senior housing in Whiting, New Jersey. Many of the residents that I hang around with grew up in North Jersey, whereas I grew up in Iowa. It's funny though because we seem to agree that movies have been a way of life for all of us. Of the six or seven of us who talk about all the movies we've seen, we unanimously agree *The Heiress* with Olivia de Havilland, Montgomery Clift and Ralph Richardson is among our top ten favorites.

CHAPTER 3

My Mother, my Sister, a Bus Ride and a Movie

Shirley, Mother, Anita, and Me heading for the bus

I don't know if I remember this event from when it actually happened or because I heard the story so often it just became real by repetition.

In my memory, my mother was five feet seven inches tall and not exactly fat, but just round. She always seemed old to me because she was forty-one when she had me, and so by comparison to the mothers of my friends she WAS old.

Our family loved movies! We went "downtown" to the movie theaters as often as somebody had enough money to pay for the cheap tickets. This particular story must have taken place sometime around three o'clock on a Wednesday afternoon. It would have been matinee day and four o'clock was the last show before the evening prices went up.

I imagine I can see it's a warm sunny day. I must have been about five years old. And my mother was dawdling as usual, going to the bathroom one more time, making sure the stove was off, looking for her pocket book and putting away the ironing board. My sister Shirley must have had a day off from high school for some reason, and she was also taking her time getting ready.

We would usually walk the seven or eight blocks downtown to save bus fare, but this day we were running late. So it was decided that if we hurried, we could catch the bus and not miss the coming attractions, cartoons and newsreels before the main feature started.

Our house was about a half block away from the bus stop, and the bus was going to be there in just a few minutes. They told me to run to the corner and ask the bus driver to wait for them. This was 1950, and no one worried about being safe crossing the street or getting kidnapped.

I got to the corner just as the bus pulled up to the bus stop sign. The driver opened the door and looked at me standing by myself, and then looked up the street and saw my sister running and my mother kind of waddling along. He smiled, and a little out of breath I asked him, "Would you please wait for my mother? She's kind of fat and can't run very fast."

As we were getting on the bus, the driver and the passengers were all smiling at me, Shirley, and my mother. I couldn't understand what was so funny. I wonder if that was the first time I unconsciously realized how nice I felt when people noticed me and liked me.

Our family told the short version of that story whenever we were in a hurry and waiting for our mother to catch up.

CHAPTER 4

My Dad, a Song, and a Movie

There were six movie theaters in Waterloo in the 1950s. The Strand, The State, The Waterloo and The Paramount were all on the East Side, and The Iowa and The Orpheum were on the West Side. They played an important part in my history of growing up in Waterloo, so much so that I can still see what they looked like inside and some of the movies I saw in them, like *Gone with the Wind* with my mom and sister-in-law Betsy at The Paramount and *To Kill a Mockingbird* at The Waterloo one afternoon sitting by myself when I was a senior in high school.

One evening when I was probably about ten, my dad and I walked to The Orpheum to see *The Hans Christian Andersen Story*. He wanted to see it, and I never did know how he knew about the author or the music or the story. But he and I walked past all the stores on the East Side, across the Fourth Street Bridge, and three more blocks to the theater; I guess it was about two miles. Now I wonder where he got enough money to spring for the evening tickets.

I have watched it on video as I got older, but I don't remember anything about it when I saw it with him. As we were walking home in the summer darkness, the most amazing thing happened.

He quietly began singing.

"Thumbelina, Thumbelina, tiny little thing"

"Thumbelina, dance, Thumbelina, sing,"

"What's the difference if you're very small?"

"When your heart is full of love, you're nine feet tall!"

He was sixty-five years old and I was ten, and I had never heard him sound so happy. It was such a surprise that I looked up at him, and he seemed different. It wasn't a word I would have known or used then, but now I realize he was transformed.

For the time it took us to walk all the way back to our house singing the chorus over and over, he was not the old, quiet, sad father I knew, but a man who sang and talked with me as if I were a grown-up girl.

Chapter 5

A Series of Movie Snapshots

Hiding in the trunk of Doris's car to get in the drive-in without paying. Making out at the drive-in with boyfriends. Watching *West Side Story* with friends while I was getting over the measles. Hoping to win something at The Paramount on "dish give-away" night. For some reason once my mother took some of my friends and me to a drive-in. Walking downtown with the Royer girls on Saturday afternoons after our chores were done to see "who knows what," just to go. Once when I was nine, we visited my sister Anita in Fresno, California, and while she was working, one afternoon my mom and dad and I went to see *Mr. Roberts* starring Henry Fonda and Jack Lemmon. Being disappointed because never once that I can remember did I ever get to sit in the balcony.

Now, I seldom go to a movie theater because I am too lazy to make the effort of driving to one and because they are so expensive. Now I watch movies on my television and miss talking and arguing with my husband about what kind of a review we would give it. Watching movies alone is not as much fun as sitting with someone and criticizing the acting or laughing at the clothes. But I still like seeing something wonderful and unexpected on film and being able to go to another place and time, forgetting I am an eighty year old woman who thinks she can still dance like John Travolta in *Saturday Night Fever*.

CHAPTER 6

The First Time I Was Ever Afraid

Admiring my new shoes

I must have been about seven years old and was very excited. My mother had promised we were going to the community center and the day had arrived. Although I had been there and I knew where it was because I passed it on my way to school every day, I didn't know exactly what happened inside.

"We are going to walk to the community center, and there is a program happening where you can play with clay and the teacher will show you how to make a bowl. We will put it on a shelf for everyone to see and I will tell them you made it. 'Isn't it pretty?' I will ask them. It will be an adventure." I was afraid I wouldn't know how to make a bowl, but if my mother said I could do it, she must be right.

"It's time to go, Emily. The flyer said it starts at 10:30, so let's get going." It was a cloudy morning and my mother looked at the sky and made a face. "I suppose I should take an umbrella in case it rains, but if it does, a little rain won't hurt us, right? And anyway we get wet when we take a bath and our clothes get wet when we wash them—so let's go. We are on an adventure like I told you!"

We walked along the street toward the community center, and as we walked my mother stopped and talked to a few of the ladies along the way. At one of the houses, she asked Mrs. Joyce the best way to cook collard greens. As we walked away I had a question for her. I don't know why it had never occurred to me to ask before. We had black neighbors, and maybe I was just used to it. Anyway, I asked why Mrs. Joyce was a different color than we were.

"It's because she is a Negro and her grandparents and great grandparents came from a faraway place called Africa. It is very hot in Africa all the time. You will learn about the countries in Africa when you get older, but right now I can tell you it's near where Jesus was born, and their skin is dark because God made them that way so they could live in the hot sun without getting sunburned. But that was a long time ago, and now some people are still that color even if they don't live there anymore. There are a lot of different shades of brown. Mrs. Joyce is one color and if you look carefully you can see all shades of brown like coffee or like milk with Hershey's Syrup. They are all pretty and different."

As we began to cross the street, I started to take my mother's hand. "You know what? Why don't you be in charge of getting us across the street safely? You hold my hand instead of me holding yours." (I just realized now as I was typing this that it was the same thing. I just thought I was in charge). "You are a big girl and know what to do." I took her hand, looked both ways, waited until all the cars were far away from us, and we walked across the street. She stooped down and kissed me and said "Good job! Now you can be trusted and will be brave enough to walk to school by yourself. I am really proud of you. You are getting bigger all the time."

My favorite part of anytime I went with my mom or dad was when we got to the railroad tracks. Today, I was lucky: "Look, there's a train switching."

That meant we might be late for our class, but it would be worth it if we could watch the big engine push and pull the railroad cars back and forth until they were in the right order for their trip to Chicago and the towns in between. There would be lots of noise as the switchmen hooked and unhooked the cars. I liked being able to say "hi" to the switchmen because I knew they knew my dad and my brother Allan. They couldn't wave because that might mean a wrong signal to the engineer.

The best part was looking for the cars that belonged to The Illinois Central Railroad.

We continued on our adventure and soon were at the community center. Today when I look at how far it was, it must have taken only a little while, but when I was six it seemed as if we had walked for at least an hour.

I had been there before and was excited about being able to walk around by myself. I knew I wasn't allowed to go outside alone, but I had permission to play in the building wherever I wanted. I waved goodbye to my mother and started to see what I could play with. I colored in a raggedy coloring book with a bunch of broken crayons. I watched some small boys trying to build a fort with Lincoln Logs. I sat with some older girls and tried to make a potholder like the ones in my mother's kitchen. They tried to help me, but I wasn't able to stretch the loops enough to get them on the loom, so I gave up.

It had been a long time since we left home and I had to go to the bathroom. Because I knew where it was and how to get there, I went in alone. It was empty, but I wouldn't need any help. When I was finished I started to try to wash my hands. But I was a little girl, the sink was high, and I was trying to climb up. I had done it before; it just took some time. While I was making my second try at getting to the faucets, a man came out of the place where the toilet was. He was about the same size as my father, but he had a dark face not like the Mrs. Joyce, who we had talked about on the way there but like he was sunburned. He had on a gray shirt with short sleeves and black pants he had forgotten to zip up.

"Can I lift you up so you can reach?" he asked.

"Yes, thank you."

"We are all alone in here and you can touch this, but don't tell anyone you did, Okay?"

I didn't know what to call it then but he put my hand on what I knew was how men went to the bathroom. His face was dark, his eyes were closed,

and I could hear him breathing. The room was no longer sunny and clear but had gotten dark and shadowy. I could not name what happened but I jumped down from the sink and started to cry. I ran out of the bathroom and up the stairs to the room where I had left my mother. I don't remember if I was crying really loud, but as I turned the corner to where she had been sitting, I saw her running towards me. She reached down and picked me up and started to cry, too.

"Emily, what's wrong? What happened? Are you hurt? Did somebody hurt you? Why are you crying so hard?" I cried till I couldn't cry anymore while my mother held me.

I was too big to carry, but she held my hand all the way home. She tucked me in bed and was still holding my hand when I woke up. When she asked me again what had happened, I was too afraid to tell her. My father came home and asked me, but I still didn't know how to say it. I just shook my head and started to cry again. I don't know why there was a man in the girl's bathroom that day, but I do know now it was the first time I was scared by a man who didn't love me.

Blond with braids who wouldn't love this girl!

CHAPTER 7

A Couple of "Pictures" I Have of my Dad and Me

Is that my Dad with me in fancy pants–where are his overalls?

The last time I went to Waterloo with my brother-in-law Frank, we took a ride through our old neighborhood. We drove by the high school I graduated from, down the street where I lived for eighteen and a half years. It was strange to see how small all the houses looked. I was sad to see the house at 227 Quincy was gone. I was told that after my parents died, the house fell into disrepair and the city tore it down as it was considered unsafe. As we drove down Fourth Street, we passed Gates Park and two memories came back to me.

Gates Park was the city park on the East Side of town. It wasn't as big or fancy as Byrnes Park on the West Side. I suppose it was because the people who lived on the West Side were richer and paid more taxes.

During that ride with Frank in 2021, the entrance was boarded up and the playground equipment was gone. All I could see was the circle in the dirt worn from the years where the grown-ups had pushed the little kids on the merry-go-round and the space where the kids had pushed themselves on the swings.

But during the summer of 1951, my dad and I would walk the six blocks to the park and he would catch me as I flew down the slide. I was old enough to make the swings work and he would sit on a bench, smoke a Pall Mall cigarette, and wait for me to be ready to be pushed on the merry-go-round.

There was no way we could make the teeter-totter work unless there was another little kid around to sit on it with me. He was six feet tall, and even though he was skinny, he was still too big to balance on it with me. When I was tired and he had smoked a couple more cigarettes, we would walk home down Lynn Street saying hello to the neighbors. They would say "Good afternoon, Mr. Engleman. How are you? How is Mrs. Engleman? Is this Emily? She gets prettier every time we see her." I would smile and say, "Thank you." We would turn the corner on Quincy Street, walk by Mrs. Lowns' house, and go in the side door of our house. My father would go upstairs and lie down for his afternoon nap.

The second park story is shorter. It takes place at the downtown Lincoln Park in Waterloo. It is still there across the street from where the old Strand Theater used to be on East Fourth Street. It takes up a whole city block. It was cool and shady with benches far enough apart from each other so people could talk quietly without being overheard.

Every once in a while, he and I walked the eight or nine blocks, sat on one of the benches facing Fourth Street, and watched the world go by. He might see someone he knew, and they would shoot the breeze for five or ten minutes. He always introduced me as his youngest daughter Emily. After they moved on, he took the time to explain how he knew the person. It was usually someone he knew from the railroad yards. As we got closer to our house, if he had enough money, we would have a root beer at the A and W. As we entered the real world again, he would go upstairs and have his nap.

This "bird-by-bird" story will be more of a chapter or two than a story. [1]I have not wanted this memoir to be just about me. I didn't just get born with no history or for no reason. I want my grandchildren to understand how their grandparents and their mother have made them who they are. Of course, it will be the job of their dad to fill in about how his family has made them who they are on Ruzicka side.

All I have added about the Engleman/Baldwin side of their DNA is just what I have found out from stories handed down by family, a few pictures, a couple of notes from 23andMe.com, and my imagination of what their lives must have been like.

So a few years ago, I sent a sample of my spit to the 23andMe company and waited to see if everything I thought I knew about my ancestors was true, or if it was just based on tales that had been told for so long that everybody assumed they were true.

I could have saved the money. All of my relatives had German and English surnames: Baldwin from my mother's English side of the family and Engleman from my father's German side. It was so obvious a friend of mine called me Frau Emily and another friend named my Netflix avatar Queen Emily long before I found out the results from 23andMe. Here they are:

99.7% European, divided into
    42.2% French and German
    25.4% British and Irish
    32.1% broken down into the rest of Northern Europe.
0.3% your guess is as good as mine.

---

[1] Bird-by-bird story: Coined by Anne Lamott in *Bird by Bird: Some Instructions on Writing and Life*, this term describes the act of choosing to write in small pieces rather than be stymied by the huge task of writing about one's entire life.

CHAPTER 8

Another Bird Shows Up

It would be such a gift if I could have Henry Louis Gates research a family tree for me, but because that isn't going to happen, some of this history will be just from stories handed down through time and some of it will be just guess work. I am almost sure there will be no kings or landowners in our family history. My ancestors would have been the people who worked in the fields and houses of the rich and famous.

My mother was born on January 19, 1904. She was christened Frederica Wilhelmina Baldwin. Her family reunions were always held in Delaware, Iowa, and I have always assumed she was either from Manchester, Iowa or Delaware, Iowa. My maternal grandmother was named Hannah Woellert Baldwin. My maternal grandfather was named Reed Baldwin. I am only guessing they were also born in that area of Iowa. My great grandparents on my mother's side were probably from somewhere in England or Ireland. She had a sister named Fern whom I am named after, but Emily, my middle name, is what everyone calls me. Fern was considered to be kind of a hell raiser. Another sister, Ruby, was supposed to be rather "saucy" according to the stories I heard about her. There was a brother George who I know nothing about.

The stories are they all drank more than a little. There were several divorces among the four of them. None of them, including my mother, would work any harder than they needed to in order to get by. My mother would plant moss roses around the front porch every summer. She loved to read. Her favorite author was Frances Parkinson Keyes, who wrote stories about New Orleans. I tried reading a few of them to honor my mom's love of them, but I never understood why she liked them so much.

CHAPTER 9

A Bird-by-Bird Story Featuring a Trip with my Mother on the *City of New Orleans*

Before you start reading this, take a minute and think of a trip you always wanted to take and never thought you would be able to take, or what trip is still on your bucket list. Mine was a trip to England and France, and I finally got there when my husband and I took a 10-day trip to London and Paris when I was fifty-five. So if you have a trip like that, you will be able to understand how grateful my mother was when she got to take me to New Orleans with her.

A visit to New Orleans had been on her bucket list ever since she became an avid reader of books by Frances Parkinson Keyes. Keyes wrote stories about New Orleans and its history and the city's culture. My mother loved the movie *A Streetcar Named Desire* by Tennessee Williams. She dreamed of riding through the French Quarter in a horse-drawn carriage. It seemed like the height of decadence to have a drink at Pat O'Brien's. She wanted to see Lake Pontchartrain and the flowers New Orleans was famous for. In 1962, her dream came true.

I have no idea how she was able to afford it. She must have been saving for a long time. Because my dad and mother worked for the Illinois Central Railroad and therefore my family could ride for free, there was no train fare, but from Chicago to New Orleans she had to pay extra because we had accommodations in a Pullman Sleeper car.

My one regret about the trip is I expect my Mom would have liked a better traveling companion. I hate to admit it, but I could have been more enthusiastic and appreciative; I remember I was kind of a pain in the ass. As the week went on, I got homesick and began to miss my friends. I think I probably was whining some of the time. I never apologized to her for my selfishness, and I hope she has forgiven me. This trip happened almost sixty years ago, so I am going to need to realize my memories are going to be hazy. Some of my "pictures" from this trip have disappeared; some are less definite and some are still vivid.

We left Waterloo on *The Land O'Corn* and changed to the *City of New Orleans* in Chicago. We were so excited. We were on our way.

I remember waking up in Memphis and looking out the top bunk of our sleeper. It must have been about midnight and the "yards" were lit with just enough light to see the shadows of the switchmen and of the mail cars being unloaded by black men who looked like they must be tired. It looked so quiet. I could see rows of freight cars on the sidings waiting to be switched to be sent on their way. It was a long layover, and my mother told me the next morning why it took so long. One of the conductors had explained that the passenger cars had to be switched to another engine to complete the trip to New Orleans.

It was early morning when we arrived in New Orleans. I have been in several train stations and can remember a little bit of each and a lot about others. Maybe because I was tired or anxious about what was going to happen next, I have no recollection of how the New Orleans station was laid out or decorated. Years later when I visited my niece in New Orleans on a cross- country train trip, I saw the train station and can remember it from that trip.

When we traveled and were going to stay for several days and had no family to stay with, we would stay at the YWCA. That is where we would stay on this trip. It was considered safe, clean, and affordable. It was convenient to the stores, museums, and coffee shops we could afford and transportation we would use if we needed to go further afield. We must have taken a cab to the "Y," and because it was too early to check in, we left our suitcases in the lobby and decided to have breakfast while we waited.

The first thing we did was find a restaurant and I got my first taste of "Southern Hospitality."

It was January and it was cold. Not cold like Iowa cold, but cold enough to have to wear a coat. I was very proud of my long black and white hounds- tooth coat I had paid for with my own money and wore it with great pleasure. That is until I heard two black waitresses make a comment about white girls showing off their new winter coats. They said it just loud enough for me to hear them. I knew they were talking about me, and I was so hurt. I wasn't showing off; I was just wearing my new coat. We sat down and ordered our breakfast and I asked my mother why they didn't think I was nice. I don't remember what she said, but it was an eye-opening welcome to the city. I was on my toes after that to make sure I didn't offend anybody. As it turned out, we were very lucky tourists.

1. We got to ride in a carriage through the French Quarter. She told me the homes and businesses were just as lovely as she had pictured them.
2. We ate beignets and drank strong, black coffee at Antoine's.
3. We took a Gray Line tour of the city so we got to see a lot of churches, Lake Pontchartrain, cemeteries with the bodies in graves above the ground, and famous New Orleans department stores. As a matter of fact, I bought a blouse and suit at Bon Marche which turned out to be the outfit I was married in.
4. I had my first legal drink at Pat O'Brien's. Because it was famous for "Hurricanes," it was probably one of those. I don't remember the effects of it, so it must not have been too strong. Also you will notice I wrote, "first legal drink," so you are right in guessing it wasn't my first drink.
5. We walked by Preservation Hall and stood outside and listened to the music, but we could not afford to go in. It was still wonderful. Somewhere during that trip I heard zydeco music and fell in love with it.
6. The high point of our trip was so unexpected that we talked about it to everyone when we got back to Waterloo. As I mentioned, we stayed at the YWCA and as was usual when the Englemans traveled anywhere, we became interested in the local people. My mother struck up a friendship with the lady who ran the front desk. I followed my mother's example and got interested in her story also. During the course of one of their conversations my mother told her new friend she would love to go to a Mardi Gras

ball. It is still hard for me to believe, but the front desk lady gave my mother two tickets to one happening in two days. I think it might have been three or four days after my birthday. It was as exciting, colorful, and jubilant as we had imagined it would be. I have a memory of a lot of vibrant green costumes, people with shiny masks, loud laughter, dancing and noise. I wonder if that woman ever knew what a contribution she made to my mother's life by giving her those two tickets. I hope so.

The trip home was only memorable because we had so much fun talking about all the things we had seen AND when we got to Chicago I found out I had measles! I traveled to Waterloo with red blotches and a mild fever. My poor mother. What a way to end the trip. But she had raised four other kids and was used to handling emergencies and staying calm.

We got back to Waterloo on a Saturday, and even though I was still covered in a few spots, on Sunday I talked my mother into letting me go to see *West Side Story* with my friends Dianne, Doris and Gloria.

An ending to a lasting memory I still hold dear after fifty-nine years.

CHAPTER 10

I Think my Mother was Courageous

When I start feeling sorry for myself for how hard I had to work when I was young, I think about what my mother had to do when she was twelve through the time she married my dad and then what she had to do when she was raising four kids through the Depression.

My mom told me she worked on the Woellert farm when she was a kid. The farm work was not as easy as it looked on *The Waltons* or *Little House on the Prairie*. Those programs just showed the mother or the kids taking a couple of clean sheets off the clothes line, not all the work that went into getting those sheets washed and dried along with everything else a family would get dirty. The kids always walked to school, but they never showed how long it took to walk there. Chickens and cows all got fed by some invisible method, certainly not by real people. At some point in every episode, the family sat down to a table filled with plates of fried chicken, mashed potatoes, green beans and two different kinds of pies, never showing all the labor it took to get that meal on the table.

Most of all, the father always had time to patiently listen to the kids' problems, hand out solutions, and make sure they knew they were loved. The mother without fail looked neat with her hair in place. Her dress was shabby of course, but clean and wrinkle-free. She was able to make dresses for her daughters and shirts for her sons and knew how to cheer them up when they were sad and scared.

My mother lived in a family where she was like the invisible person who made it possible for families like the Waltons to be able to solve all their problems in an hour.

I am finding out how painful it is going to be to give up my "stories" of how mean she was to me, blaming her for not protecting me better. I am going to be angry. I didn't know I had a choice in how to look at those "stories."

I have only a vague idea of what she wanted as a young woman. She was forty-one when I was born, so she was maybe fifty-five or fifty-six when she started to share with me bits and pieces of how she became the woman I knew. What were her dreams and what did she settle for; did she ever cry when she was alone and tired? Did she read the stories of New Orleans and go to the movies so often to escape the sadness of lost dreams and disappointments? I am sure that's true. Oh, how I wish she were here now, so I could tell her how sorry I am for the terrible things I said to her when I was a teenager. I would thank her for giving me the courage to go to California when I was only eighteen. It hurt her so much when I left home, and I only figured that out quite recently.

I don't know how to start, so I guess I will just let the stories go by as if we are watching a movie. She was a "liberal" long before I ever knew what that meant. She was thoughtful, tactful, kind and funny.

She was a white woman who joined the NAACP in 1955 at a time and place where it was not "the thing to do." We lived in a neighborhood that by that time had been integrated and my mother could never understand why some people thought that it was wrong to enjoy neighbors who were a different color. Mr. and Mrs. Joyce's family lived across the street from us. Mrs. Spencer and her family lived in the house where the Lowns had lived. Mr. and Mrs. Parham's family lived on the right side of our house.

Looking back on it, I wonder if our neighbors really enjoyed her company, or did they tolerate her presence because she was white and they didn't want to offend her. I don't think there was any thought on her part that she might be acting like she was patronizing them or being Mrs. Benevolent White Lady. My sisters and I visited the Quincy Street neighborhood after my mother and father had both died and had coffee with one of her next door friends. We sat with the lady of the house and reminisced about my parents with her. She laughed and said our mother made better collard greens than she did. What a lovely compliment from a lady who knew all there was to know about Southern cooking!

My mother had friends in the black community that we would visit. I loved to sit and listen to the talk and the laughter. The only time I ever heard her make a comment to me was the first time we went to see her friends who were black. I was about six years old and she told me, "Don't say anything if the children want to touch your hair. They will be interested because it's different from theirs." The only reason she said anything was so the kids wouldn't be embarrassed if I asked them why they wanted to do that.

Thinking about it today as I write this, I was aware that the people we knew on Quincy Street and the families who met us as we walked downtown always addressed my parents as Mr. and Mrs. and my ma and dad would address them the same way. I can only assume her friends were not that formal, although I can't say for sure.

I grew up and continue to be very proud of my family and my mother, especially that they all taught me how not to be afraid of people who are different than I am. That does not mean that I have to like everybody or admire everybody's point of view; it did, however, teach me to be tolerant. Now all those stories I have told do not mean our family was perfect. I am ashamed of the next couple of stories. You can judge me as harshly as you want because I judge myself just as much as you could judge me. My only defense is I didn't know any better, and when I found out how terrible it was, I never did it again.

I am even humiliated to admit this but it is part of my story, so please forgive me.

When I was growing up, my mother always had cats. She tolerated a really mean Siamese at one time. I was afraid of it the whole time she had it. I don't remember what happened to it; I expect the devil came and got it and took it to hell to show newcomers what they had in store. Anyway, when I was maybe five or six we had an all-black cat whose name was Nig, and when the Joyce family moved into the house across the street from us, my mother said we would have to rename it. I didn't understand why until it was explained to me what it meant. I wonder why my mother allowed the name in the first place.

Here is another thing I wish had never happened. Our house was several blocks away from an area where the houses ended and farm land began. Once in a while I would take a ride in that area with my parents and some relative or other, and someone would ask about the very large rocks scattered on the ground. "They are called "nigger toes" aren't they?" someone once asked. Then when the kids would play in that area that's what we called them too. Looking back, I am more than sorry now.

CHAPTER 11

Here is a Story about Me and One More about My Mother

My dad was a patient in a hospital for the mentally ill for a period of time when I was about ten. He had been seriously hurt in an accident when I was three, and as a result of that accident he would from time to time get violent. My mother explained that the treatment he received caused severe headaches. She was unable to handle his outbursts of rage and had to commit him for the help she couldn't give him.

The older kids were out of the house by then and so it was just her and me. My memories of that time are pretty vague. I don't know if she worked or how she supported us. Once my brother John told me our church helped us with paying some of the bills and with groceries. I suppose that is probably true, but I have no idea if that's so. This story happened once when my dad was away during one of the times he was being treated for his mental problems. My parents' bedroom was on the first floor and because it was just my mom and me, I got to sleep in the upstairs front bedroom which had always been used by my sisters. When I found out I was going to get to be upstairs by myself, I felt so grown-up.

The first few nights it was exciting being alone and having a full-size bed all to myself. I could listen to a little radio next to my bed. I could read until I got tired and had the windows open to hear the night sounds through the trees. I especially loved to hear the sounds the cars made as they went by on the rough pavement of our street. After a while, it was lonely being all by myself, but I didn't want to admit it. I woke up one night and all of a sudden I was scared. I don't know why, but I started to cry because I was alone. All I could think of was getting downstairs and seeing my mother. It was just a few steps to the hallway and the light switch and the stair steps. I can't remember if I ran down the ten steps or if I walked slowly because I felt I had to be quiet. All I was aware of was feeling safe as I opened the door into the dining room. I saw the shapes of the big table and the stand with the telephone on it. The light from the streetlamp was shining through the front room window and I knew where I was. I must have still been crying a little because when I pushed back the curtain to my mother's bedroom I saw my mother, she was sitting up in bed and asking me, "Emily, what's the matter? Are you sick?"

Looking back on it, I wonder why I wasn't surprised when our neighbor sat up in bed next to my mother. It seemed so normal to see our black friend Mr. Johnson wide awake next to my mother. I said hello to him and he said hello to me all very matter-of-fact.

"All right, Emily, say goodnight and I will go upstairs with you and sit with you until you go back to sleep." And that's what happened. Nothing was ever said about it, then, in the morning, or ever. It never occurred to me to ask her about why he was in bed with her or wonder why I didn't think it was strange. I must have thought it was okay.

I guess if anything, I was happy she had someone who was kind and helped her feel cared for. All these years later, I wonder if I was just happy the constant arguing had stopped.

I am not judging any part of that time. She was probably only fifty years old, and my dad had been in the hospital for months I suppose. She must have been lonely with only me to keep her company. Mr. Johnson was a friend and neighbor, and she must have felt safe with him. I don't know. All I know for sure is they never talked about it or made it seem as if there was anything to be ashamed of.

There came a time when I was in tenth grade that I became a friend and admirer of another tenth grader who lived near me. I can't remember his last name, but his first name was Bobby. I really liked him because he could make me laugh and he was nice to me. He would call me on the phone once in a while and we would talk about school and our friends. I was shy and scared of the big high school we were going to. I wore second-hand clothes from the Salvation Army, so I knew I would never be one of the popular kids. I lived on the "wrong side of the tracks," so his friendship meant a lot to me. I don't know how it happened. It must have been very subtle, but one afternoon we were walking home together and I got a feeling I wasn't going to be able to be friends with Bobby anymore. Suddenly I realized because I was white and Bobby wasn't, there were lots of people who thought that was somehow wrong. Where did that idea come from? We had neighbors who were black, and I was so surprised people might not like me because Bobby was my friend.

Our black neighbors helped my dad around the house because he was old and needed help. I thought I was friends with Andrea Joyce who lived across the street. Her brother Ronnie didn't like me, but I thought that was because I was a girl. Could there have been another reason?

What could that reason be and what could I do about it? I am sure I never thought to myself, "I don't care if they don't like me. He is my friend and I will stay friends with him." How was I going to be able to explain to him that my other friends' opinions were more important to me than his friendship was when I didn't understand it myself? I never wanted to hurt anyone because I knew how bad I felt when I was hurt.

CHAPTER 12

Movin' on Down the Road

Our family loved any kind of transportation: planes, trains, second-hand automobiles, city buses, Greyhound buses–never motorcycles–Navy ships, streetcars, taxis. Sometimes, only our imaginations or our feet took us away from the house on Quincy Street in Waterloo to see a world we dreamed of.

That is the only reason I can think of why everyone in my family loves to travel. There might have been a stagecoach driver in our history and going back so far as the cave men and women, our ancestors may have been the people who sat around the fire and wished someone would invent the wheel. My mother's father, Reed Baldwin, and my father, John Engleman, worked as switchmen for many years in Waterloo, Iowa for the Illinois Central Railroad. My brothers John and Allan did not make careers with the railroad but worked there as teenagers doing whatever they could. My mother Freda worked on the switchboard part-time. It was really such a benefit because we could travel on what was called a pass with no charge as long as we made reservations ahead of time. I just now realized it let us know ahead of time that we were going somewhere.

My mother had aunts and uncles in Manchester and Delaware, little towns about fifty miles from Waterloo. She grew up working on a farm with these people, and every once in a while she would get homesick. I would come downstairs all ready to go to school and she would tell me, "We are going to see 'the aunts' today, so you can stay home." No warning, just a surprise visit. My dad would put on a clean pair of overalls. I would change into jeans, put my school books on the dining room table, and we would be ready to go.

My mother, however, had a longer routine before she would be ready. First she had to feed the cat, go to the bathroom, take off her apron, and go to the cellar for jars of jelly for presents for whoever we ended up seeing. Then she had to make sure the stove was off and the windows were open or closed depending on the forecast for rain. Then she had to change her housedress for something a little nicer, put on her hat, find her purse, go to the bathroom one more time, lock the side door, and finally we would be ready to go. When I was growing up, my mother always drove wherever we went. I guess she must have been a good driver because as far as I know, she never had an accident or got a ticket.

I just turned eighty, and so these memories are over seventy years old. The old Route 20 that ran from Waterloo to Manchester was two very narrow lanes and probably followed the original Indian trails. There were no interstates or even a four lane highway, but I loved that ride. I always looked forward to seeing the big turn just before we got to Jesup, and then there was a barn I was sure would have blown over since the last time we went by, but it was always still standing when we stopped going on that road. For all I know, it's still there breathing its last waiting for the next Iowa tornado to topple it to the ground.

The halfway point was Independence, which was twenty-five miles from where we left, with twenty-five miles to go before we got to the high hill in Manchester where the aunts lived. As I mentioned in an earlier story, there was a mental hospital in Independence, but it was not called that. In hushed voices it was called "the insane asylum," and I think I was always just a little worried that an inmate would escape, jump in our car, and demand us to take him to some dilapidated old house in the woods someplace.

The scary part was worth the excitement when I could look forward to the trip home. Would we stop at the ice cream shop before we went home? It was always an unspoken question because if I asked, the answer would be no. I just had to wait and hope to see if the car would turn into the driveway when we drove by. If the answer was yes, it wasn't good to get excited and start yelling hurray. If the answer was no, there was no disappointment and crying about it. More often than not, we stopped. Looking back, the difference between stopping and not stopping was probably if there was any extra money in my mother's pocketbook.

The first house we would stop at was my Aunt Martha's. She lived on the main street near the stores and the businesses. I liked that one the best because when the grownups started to talk about the relatives and gossip about who was doing what with whom, my mother would ask me if I wanted to take a walk "downtown" and look around. I Loved That! In those days it was safe for an eight year old to be alone among strangers, and I was never afraid. Of course I was never really alone because everyone on the street had their eyes on me and knew who I belonged to. I guess my dad must have been outside smoking to get away from the women.

When I got tired of looking in all the store windows and wondering why there were two dentists in such a little town and watching the barber pole stripes go around, I would go back to a breakfast of homemade rolls and jam with real butter, peaches and plums from the jars "put up" during the summer. After a twenty minute "Iowa Goodbye," it would be time to move on to the next visit with another Aunt Martha. This one was also my favorite because she was a hugger and called me "her little 'sucka upple,'" which besides meaning "sugar apple" in German, in English it's an unspoken "I love you and you are precious to me." Her hugs meant unconditional love and acceptance.

Now would be another meal; this one was much more elaborate because it would be a traditional farm dinner. Even if there were only my dad and four or five women at the meal, there would be enough in case four or five farm hands that used to sit at the dinner table would miraculously reappear with huge appetites after working in the fields all morning. Should I list or leave out all the parts of this meal, assuming you know what would be there? Maybe you have never seen or read *O Pioneers* by Willa Cather. If you haven't, I absolutely recommend it. There would be three kinds of meat, mashed potatoes, three vegetables, including fresh cucumbers and fresh tomatoes, pickles, homemade rolls, lemonade and three kinds of pies. My favorite part would always be the pies!

Then it was three o'clock and we had one more stop to make at my Aunt Dorey's. Because she lived several miles out of town, our "Iowa Goodbye" started at 3:20 so we would have time to visit and have another meal to hold us until we got back to Waterloo. This visit was different because she actually lived on a farm. I think she must have had grown children helping her; even though it was a small farm by then, it would have been too much for her to do on her own.

At the first Aunt Martha's, most of the furniture had been moved from the big farmhouse into the small apartment in town, so everything was pretty crowded. The grown-ups would sit at the big dining room table and drink coffee and gossip, and I would sit and listen in a giant padded living room chair next to the table. I liked hearing them laugh at the time Mrs. Smith walked into church with her hat on backwards and then they had to make her feel better, so three of the ladies put theirs on backwards. They cried when the talk turned to how sad it was when another of Mrs. Smith's daughters had a second miscarriage. I was hidden in the folds of the big chair and they forgot I was there, so I learned about how funny and kind women could be and how critical they sometimes could be, also.

I would eavesdrop and then get sleepy as I watched the clock with the golden balls go around only so far and then turn back all by themselves and then start around again. Then it would be time for my mother to wake me up and send me on my walk. At my Aunt Dorey's farm one time, it was high summer when we had gone for our unexpected ride and by the time we got to her house we had our late supper outside. The farm buildings stood out in high relief against the sky as the sun set low. It was warm, quiet and calm. There were remnants of the bologna sandwiches on the table along with some potato salad and some uneaten cookies that would get wrapped up and sent home with us. Suddenly the quiet of the scene was interrupted by an ungodly squawking. The geese had gotten loose and were making a run for the crumbs on the ground. I started yelling and trying to run away, but one of the farm hands picked me up and as far as I was concerned saved my life.

All the talking, laughing and card playing were done for this trip and it was time for our final "Iowa goodbye." This would have to be the longest one because we didn't know when the next visit was going to be and we didn't want to leave until we had said everything we needed to say until next time. I have never been able to just get up and leave when it was time to go. It's a foreign concept to just get up, say goodbye, and walk out the door. It must be possible, though, because I have seen people do it.

The ride home was quiet and I knew there would be no ice cream stop this trip. We had eaten pretty much all day and it was getting dark. I had a lot to think about and remember, so I wasn't too disappointed. The old barn was still standing. Now the little towns were going in the opposite direction and I knew we were getting close to home. When we pulled into the driveway on Quincy Street, all that was left for me to do was carry the packages we had been sent home with into the house, say good night to my parents, and go to bed. I would dream about the magic clock, the barber pole, the geese and the hug from my Aunt Martha, close my eyes, and wait for the next time my mother would tell me as I came down the stairs, "No school today. We are going to see the aunts."

CHAPTER 13

Pictures from the Trips I Can Recall

I am certainly not the only person who understands why traveling can teach more about life than what goes on in your family or neighborhood. There is some foreshadowing in the next few paragraphs so the opening sentences will show what's coming.

These stories are about how grown-ups who had just met necked on a train during the late hours of an overnight trip. How to get really embarrassed and live to tell the story. How to handle a full service meal in a dining car. How to be the center of attention and not be a brat. Figuring out how to sleep comfortably in a coach seat. I had learned by example from my parents how to behave in public: how to listen, how to answer, how to be kind and most of all how to be interested in people.

1. Pulling into the Illinois Central train station in Chicago at 12:45 p.m. and knowing this time we would hit the corner of the building. (We never did.)
2. Being given permission to ride the station escalator as often as I wanted by myself.
3. Wishing I could explain how beautiful the station was with its many rows of dark benches, dim lights, high ceilings, so many people wearing so many colors, and how noisy it would be with all the murmuring voices and the cries of people greeting their visitors as they came into the station.

4. Finally getting outside and walking by Marshall Fields. Deciding which museum to visit on this trip: the Natural History Museum, the Field Museum or the Adler Planetarium, my favorite. The way I remember it, most of these were in downtown Chicago, but the Museum of Science and Industry was some distance away and we would have to take the El.

5. Once my mother and I took the train from Waterloo to Fort Dodge and stayed overnight in a hotel. I don't know why. Just a whim I suppose.

6. A couple of day trips to Galena, Illinois where my mother and father were married and many years later my sister Anita and her husband Frank were also married. I was fifteen years old and Frank's "best man"; I cried through the ceremony because I was happy Anita was getting married to a good guy and my nieces would have a dad.

7. More than a few train trips to Manchester to stay with some cousins on their farm for a week during the summer. Once I went with my best friend, Joan, and the cousins, Joan, and I stood around the piano and sang in harmony, "The Wayward Wind" by Gogi Grant.

8. On one of those trips to Chicago, an unexpected friendship was started. Judy Thein and her mother were going to Chicago on the same train as my mother and I. So the mothers sat together and Judy and I sat next to each other. Our friendship started that day and lasted until Judy died a couple of years ago. We lived on the same street but had never met because she went to St. Mary's Catholic School and I went to Immanuel Lutheran.

She became a big part of my life because we lived so close to each other and were the same age. She had lots of friends that lived near her, and my friends were scattered around town. Plus, she had brothers and sisters who were part of our lives too. I owe her and her family a lot for being my friends and companions as I was growing up. Once we made taffy that turned into an all day, very hot, expensive and sticky project that we ended up throwing away. Her older brother Tom had friends that at one time or another we all had crushes on.

CHAPTER 14

We Started in Waterloo with a Final Stop in Fresno

This short story is about the only time I went on a long trip with both my mother and father. This particular train ride took place in1954; by then I was nine years old and much more alert as to what was going on and why.

It was a wonderful time and I suppose it's where I got my first taste of how much of an adventure train travel could be.

Train travel in the 1950's was much more glamorous than it is today. Now you are lucky if you can get a box lunch instead of going to the dining car with real linen tablecloths, as in the past. The backrests of the coach seats had red pieces of linen on them so the men wouldn't get them all grunged up with Brylcreem. The reason I am going into this detail is because I want to explain the difference between now and then in the ladies' restrooms. You know what I am talking about when I describe airplane restrooms? They are smaller than the old telephone booths and a lot dirtier. Well the restrooms on trains are now like that, too.

The cars on *The Zephyr*, which was the name of the train we were on during this particular trip, were right out of a Hollywood movie. If you've ever seen *North by Northwest* with Cary Grant and Eva Marie Saint, it was like that. Anyway the ladies' restrooms were, well, the only word I can use to describe them is "opulent." One wall was covered in mirrors and with little velvet covered stools in front of the mirrors. Lush green carpets and chandeliers made them look like a French chateau, or at least what I imagine one would look like.

When I got tired of walking up and down the passenger cars, I would go into one of the ladies' rooms and watch the women come in and fix their hair and makeup. And I wonder how some of them looked so glamorous, but a lot of them looked like my mother! I wonder if it ever occurred to me then like it does now that I was glad my mother looked kind and quiet, and the rich ladies looked like they might never hug their daughters when they were scared and confused. Oh well, probably not.

I was treated as a grown-up and let loose to roam the passenger cars as much as I wanted. No one could kidnap me or get off a moving train, and there were only so many places I could be hidden! I don't think I would have been allowed to go in the Pullman cars, but I must have had some sense they were off limits and luxurious. Now that I think of it, I must have seen them in Hollywood movies. I had wandered through one of the next cars and became friends with a young woman; she was maybe eighteen or so, and we kept each other company for awhile. I had her full attention until a sailor–yeah, you guessed it–in his "blues" boarded the train somewhere in Nebraska, I guess. They started talking and were involved with each other the rest of the trip. My new friend was kind, however, and so was the sailor because neither of them told me to get lost.

I had been asleep for what must have been a long time, and the people in the car had mostly gone to sleep too or were trying to. The lights were all off except for a couple of reading lights aimed at the laps of the people doing their best to get interested in something other than the darkness outside the windows. I don't know how it happened that I was facing my new friends, but I was stretched out across two seats and could see everything going on across from me. My new friends were now very good friends with each other. As long as I pretended to still be asleep, I could watch them and understand what "making out" meant. I kept my eyes half open and watched for a while. They never got too much further than I did when I did the same thing on a bus to California when I was eighteen. I went back to sleep, and the next morning the three of us had breakfast. I went back to my seat when they stopped paying attention to me.

One final episode about this train ride and then one more story of what happened in the Los Angeles train station.

CHAPTER 15

Some Things Could Have Been Finer in the Diner

We didn't have every meal in the dining car because it was expensive, so sometimes we would share a sandwich from the club car. Other times when the train stopped, we could get off the train for a time and vendors with homemade regional foods would meet the train. This food was always delicious: burritos or rice with savory sauces and soups were just some of the unexpected meals we could take back to the observation car. We could watch the world go by as we ate the kind of food we never got in Iowa.

Breakfast was a lot of food for the money, so twice we ate eggs, toast, juice, bacon (my favorite), and of course two sausage patties the size of a half dollar, maybe a banana or a tangerine, and several cups of good, hot, strong coffee.

Because there were not a lot of tables, there were three seatings; you were asked when you boarded which one you preferred. We almost always got the one we wanted because the head waiter knew from our tickets we were a railroad family. This little extra perk made us feel special.

My mother must have been saving for just an occasion, and the second night we had asked for the second seating because it would be crowded and we could watch a larger number of people. I was waiting to see who the fourth person at our table would turn out to be. All I can remember was a man, and the meal was certainly some kind of a beef entree. When I was nine, I had never heard the word "entree" but learned it later.

Everything was going along pretty well. My mom must have looked especially nice with her black dress and silver necklace. Her hair was curled and beautifully gray. (I inherited my lovely gray hair from her but it was never curly.) My dad had to have put on his best flannel plaid shirt. He had two IC railroad caps: one to wear to the "yards" and one for company. This was the company one. My skirt was my best one. For sure it was cotton, ironed, and starched with a matching blouse.

1946, Mother and Father

My parents were listening to the talk about our tablemate's job, and my dad was probably explaining where the next stop would be. I was watching a pretty lady walking by our table. She looked like a movie star, tall with pretty hair and black stockings and black, really high heels. I wanted to get a good look at the shoes because they were so different from the kind my mother wore.

I leaned over as she was walking by and just kept going until I was on the floor with my skirt all bunched underneath me. The chair was on its side. The lady had turned around and was looking at me like "what just happened?" Two people at the table closest to me were laughing. My dad was trying to figure out what was the matter, and I started to cry because I was so embarrassed. Ma was trying to help me up.

That's what happened on the night my mother had saved up for so long, and I knew I had ruined it. It wasn't ruined for her, but she felt so bad for me because I thought I had made a mess of things. She never mentioned it again, and the next morning we all laughed about what the lady must have been thinking when she saw me on the floor and wondered how I had ended up there. I am sure she never imagined it was because of my fascination with her shoes.

CHAPTER 16

A Medical Report From the L.A. Train Depot with Background (1954)

I don't know how old I was when the yearly bouts with tonsillitis started, but they ended when I was in 10th grade and had my tonsils removed. I was kind of looking forward to the operation because I was tired of every winter knowing I was going to have a sore throat for a week, and I was assured that would end after "I was healed!!" I was, however, afraid it would stop me from getting excused from swimming during gym class. I was in a big public school in Iowa where physical education was a requirement for graduation. Kids were expected to play basketball, baseball, football or golf if they were rich, or they could run track or swim.

I couldn't play any of those for a variety of reasons. I was too gangly for basketball, and I couldn't stop myself from throwing the bat when I would get a hit in baseball. My teammates waited in the dugout when I was up to bat, and I was always picked last on whatever team was unfortunate enough to have to make the last choice. I don't think any of them were mean enough to start counting ahead of time to see if it would be them. Anyway, golf and football would not work as a team sport for me because for one, I was and still am a girl, and I wasn't then or now for that matter, rich.

I would get out of breath if I had to run too far. I wasn't popular or cute enough to be a cheerleader. I had never learned how to swim. That, however, was not the reason I wasn't on the swim team. I ALWAYS got a cold and a sore throat if my ears got water in them, which happened if people were on the swim team. You saw that coming, right? So, I always had an excuse. Our family doctor, who had graduated from medical school in "19 aught four" as my father used to say, would be asked in August before school started to sign a doctor's note saying I couldn't take part in the swim classes and explaining why not. I am not sure how my mother explained the reason for keeping me out of swimming after I had had my tonsils out, but she did. One more added benefit was I never had to wear the ugly, green shapeless swimsuits the girls had to wear.

So now we are back to 1954 running through the Los Angeles train station to catch a connecting train. When I tell this story to an audience I can never know if we were on our way to San Diego to see my brother or to Fresno to see my sister. Incidentally, all I can remember about San Diego is that it is where I had my first nectarine and fell in love with a new kind of fruit. And also incidentally, in Fresno is where two outstanding events occurred. It was the first time I ate a California hamburger, which is a slice of cheese on a double hamburger with fresh lettuce, fresh, sliced tomatoes, and onions. Also one afternoon when my sister was working, my mother, father and I went to see the movie *Mr. Roberts* with Henry Fonda and Jack Lemmon. Food and movies all on the same trip and spending time with relatives. What could be better?

But once more, I digress. We were running through the train station so we wouldn't miss our connecting train, and I suddenly had to stop because I couldn't stop coughing. I just stood in the middle of all these people walking by and looking at me. My mother and father couldn't do anything to help me stop. There were two people from a train crew calling for help. I just could not stop. I don't know how long it went on, but it seemed like a long time. I was so scared because I wasn't able to catch my breath. Even as I write this all these years later, I can still feel I need to take a few deep breaths.

I don't know how my coughing fit resolved itself, but we didn't miss our train. I must have finally gradually stopped coughing, and my mother stopped looking so worried because she saw I was better.

CHAPTER 17

Broadway, Here I Don't Come

It seems as if when I was growing up there were always a bunch of kids in my neighborhood. Becky Lown's grandmother lived next door to my house. Becky's grandmother had a running feud with my mother, and I never did know why except there were a few people my mother had a feud with for unknown reasons. So one winter afternoon, Becky invited me to come over to spend the afternoon with her and keep her company. It's boring when your grandmother is an old lady and won't do fun stuff like play in the laundry room and plug up the sink so water runs all over the floor and you can't make it stop.

That's what we did that afternoon. Being the coward I was, I ran home and left my friend to take the blame by herself. I don't know for sure, but my mother's reaction when I told her that I did it, and Mrs. Lown was probably really mad, was to say, "It serves her right, the old battle ax. Now she will have to clean that room, and it's about damn time." (I added the "damn" for comic effect. My mother would not have said that–not because she was a prude, but she only used language like that when she was provoked.)

Mary Akers and her sister Sheila lived two blocks away. She and I were good friends and would leave May baskets on each other's doors on May Day. I visited her in Iowa City once after she and her family moved there. I stayed with my father's half brother and his wife and felt very grown up because I was allowed to go by myself.

The Joyce family lived across the street, and the thing that made them famous was they were the first black family to move into the neighborhood.

Incidentally, there was no uproar when that happened. They were always so kind and gracious to us and their daughter Andrea, if not a playmate because she was two years older than I was, tolerated me and included me when her friends came to see her.

After I had moved to California and my sister and her family were living in Washington, Mr. and Mrs. Joyce made sure my dad had meals and was still on his way to the yards every day after my mother was put in a nursing home. Their son, Ronnie, mowed the lawn and took the trash cans to the curb for him. I found that out from my sister Anita and my brother-in-law Frank when they would come to Waterloo and talk with the neighbors about how Mr. Engleman was getting along. My dad would tell Anita, "Mrs. Joyce sent over supper for me last night." "What was it?" Anita would ask. "I don't remember, but it was really good, I know that!"

Thank you to all of the neighbors who were so good to my parents. Thank you for taking over the care I could have provided had I stayed in Iowa. That was sixty-two years ago, and I have tears in my eyes remembering how kind you all were to them while they lived among you.

In addition to the names I've mentioned—Becky Lown and her crabby grandmother and the Joyce family who had kids who tolerated me and had parents who taught them to be kind—two more sets of kids played a big part in the kind of neighborhood I grew up in.

There were the Royers, and I don't know if I ever knew the last name of the other family. There were, however, a bunch of boys and girls in each family. I never did get straight who all the second family kids were. The second family is the one that played a part in why I named this chapter about Broadway. The Royer girls and a couple of the boys showed me what it was like to have a time in my life with no cares and no fears of the unexpected. As I try to figure out this timeline, I am confused about what happened when and how old I was.

Let's just say it all happened because it did. The sun shone every day. There was enough money so all four of us girls could walk downtown and get a nickel cherry coke at Kresge's and walk home trying to figure out if there was a dime left for an ice cream cone. I don't think there ever was, but it was exciting to think about. As we got older we could go to the Gates Park pool and pretend we were Esther Williams. One summer, trampolines were really popular. On the corner of Quincy Street and 4th

Street in Waterloo, a half block from my house, five big holes were dug and trampolines were stretched over them. My friend Judy (from the train story) would come over; she, the three Royer girls and I each put in a dime, so for fifty cents we could all pretend we knew what we were doing for fifteen minutes. If there was no one waiting, the guy running the place would let us jump longer.

I don't know why this particular afternoon is so clear in my memory, but when I think of the Royer family, this is the day I think of.

The girls were in the house spying on two of the boys from the upstairs balcony until they heard us laughing at them. They hollered at us and told us to get downstairs. The next thing all six of us were sitting quietly outside on an old splintery picnic table. All of us were looking out in the same direction at the same sight: a long row of sunflowers Mrs. Royer had planted that spring. The afternoon sun was directly overhead and was blinding us with the yellow and green of the giant flowers. It was a wonderful, serene, precious moment. The spell was broken when all at the same time we heard a bird singing. We all looked at each other without saying a word as we realized we had seen something we couldn't explain.

CHAPTER 18

Broadway, Here I Come

I lived at 227 Quincy Street until I left for California when I was not quite nineteen. When this story takes place I am probably about ten. There was temporarily only one bunch of kids who lived near me around the corner on Linn Street. I could get to their house by running through Mrs. Lown's backyard if she wasn't home. Otherwise I had to run around the corner on the sidewalk.

At ten, I was the oldest and the other kids were just a little younger, maybe five through eight. I guess they must have been brothers and sisters and cousins because there was an assortment of ages that couldn't have all been living in that little house. I don't remember a lot of adult supervision there because I never saw any grown-ups. There was a swing set in the backyard with one swing and a slide and a seesaw in name only. A bike or two with the paint mostly gone and a baseball bat and glove some older kid had left stuck in the dirt. We all would just sit on the front porch of their house and talk about who knows what, and pretty soon my mother would call me home so I could help with something. I don't know why but at some point I got the idea they were (if I had known the word then, I would have described them as unsavory!) maybe just a little scary.

They didn't come over to my front porch very often, but one afternoon I invited five or six of the youngest ones to come over because I would be conducting a funeral. (I knew how to do this because I had been going

51

to a Lutheran church since I was a baby and knew how to act in church. Unlike, as it turned out at the service, some of the mourners, who did not.)

My turtle had died and I had the casket decorated, the prayers were written and the hymns were ready to go. Now all I needed was a congregation to hear me preach about what a good pet he had been and how sad I was that he was dead.

Looking back it was probably like a lot of funerals where the minister didn't know the deceased because I have no idea where that turtle came from or how and why he was in my care—well, maybe not so much my care if he was dead. Anyway, he was more than likely a giveaway from Kresge's and I won him because I knew the other word for turtle. I also would have had no idea how I knew that.

So the stage is set. I was wearing one of my mother's old black house dresses. The congregation was seated on the front steps of the house. I was standing as tall and straight as I could on the top of the steps looking down from behind the cardboard box altar. It had been adorned with an old white dish towel with a yellow cross drawn on it.

I sang a verse of "Jesus Loves Me," said a made up prayer, and then began my recollection of my time with the deceased. It must have gone something like this. "We are gathered here to say goodbye to a dear friend of mine. His name was Keith. I have known him for a long time. He lived in a glass bowl in my bedroom and ate grass and drank water. He kept me company while I did my schoolwork."

"Hey you guys on the bottom step, settle down. Don't you know you're in church? Bring that slingshot up here. You'll get it back after we bury my friend."

"Now be quiet because I'm going to tell you how he came to live with me last year. He must have lived on a farm near Cedar Falls because when I found him on my back porch, he was in a little box with the words 'Property of True Value Hardware Store, Main Street, Cedar Falls.' I think he must have been blown here during that last tornado that went through. Anyway his family was dead, we guess, and now he was an orphan. I wouldn't want to be an orphan and not know where my family is, would you?"

"I asked you all a question. Would you want to be an orphan and have to live with a bunch of strangers and eat a lot of strange food? I know I wouldn't, and Keith wouldn't either."

(Now my voice was getting softer and a little quavery. The girls stopped giggling and the boys stopped punching each other.)

"He was all alone and I took him in and kept him warm and gave him plenty to eat and drink, and he was happy."

"I am so sad he died because now who will keep me company and watch me sleep? He was such a good friend and now he's gone. Maybe he will find his brothers and sisters in heaven. But I will miss him."

Now it was very quiet on the steps and I was crying a little and so were a few of the little kids. One of the big boys had his arm around his little brother and I heard him say, "Don't worry, we are too big to get carried away in a tornado."

I had them right where I wanted them, so I let them all cry a minute longer and then I raised my voice and said, "We will all stand now and I'll sing one verse of 'Onward Christian Soldiers.'"

"Please follow me to the back yard where I've dug a hole for his casket. Each of you can put a spoonful of dirt on his grave and say goodbye to him if you want. Don't forget to do this quietly as a sign of respect. Then you can all go home."

I guess I didn't have enough authority for that to happen. But they were pretty quiet as they ran away.

I've watched a lot of performers talk about that moment when they realized they loved it when they were in front of an audience and could make them laugh and cry. Well, that was the moment for me at ten years old. I was conscious of the way I had talked and cried. I could move those kids to feel what I felt. I wondered if I could do that when I got older.

I am having a hard time getting going with this part of my history because it has been so important to me. Performing has always been easy for me. Just before it's time to walk on stage is scary as hell, but once I can remember the first line, I am okay. When I was in fifth grade at Immanuel Lutheran School, I had the lead in the end of the school year play and we were almost at the end of the performance. Parents, relatives, teachers, the principal and the rest of the school were the audience. Everything was going along as planned when suddenly no one on stage was talking. What was happening? It was so quiet. I heard one of the teachers backstage whispering, "Emily, it's your line." I knew that, but I didn't remember my name let alone the line. Everybody on stage just stood there and looked at me. The boy next to me whispered, too. "Just say it, Emily." I was frozen. Now the teacher who was telling me what to say came to the edge of the curtain and said loudly enough for everybody in the two front rows to hear. "Emily, say (whatever it was supposed to be.)" It wasn't Shakespeare, probably something like "Look, here comes the hunter and his dog."

I woke up and shouted, "LOOK, HERE COMES THE HUNTER AND HIS DOG!!" Everybody breathed again and it was over, and everybody clapped and stood up and had coffee and cake.

I'm surprised I ever wanted to act again. The thing is I was really lucky; I had no choice. I always got the leads because in a small school I had the loudest voice and the best memory, with the exception of the aforementioned time.

At this point I would like to list the number of times since Keith's burial and the hunter and his dog episode that I've been lucky enough to be in front of an audience. There were community theater productions, high school plays, and summer plays where we rehearsed at the same community building where the man in the bathroom scared me. Church talent shows, only once singing "Hit The Road, Jack," and doing karaoke, which was a disaster and scarred me for life of ever trying that again.

My friend Judy and I talked more than once about going to New York City after we graduated from high school. We could get an apartment together and we would become famous. Judy's invitation to her family for opening night at the Metropolitan Opera House would become an heirloom to display on the mantle of the house on Fourth Street. My playbill celebrating some undisclosed new play by Tennessee Williams would be in one of the display cases at East High School in Waterloo. "LOCAL GRADUATE, EMILY ENGLEMAN, HAS LEAD IN BROADWAY HIT OPENING CHRISTMAS EVE IN NEW YORK CITY." It was our dream, and at some level I think we really thought it might happen. And we also knew at a more realistic level that we would become what we had been programmed to be.

Judy got married soon after graduation in a traditional Catholic ceremony. I was not Catholic, so I wasn't able to be in the wedding party, but I did get to be in charge of making sure people signed the guest book. We stayed in touch for all the years of our friendship, and when I visited Waterloo every other year to see my family, I would stay with Judy. The visits always included talking about our high school boyfriends. On one of our Waterloo visits, she took Michele and me to get our ears pierced so I could look "fancy" for my 20th year class reunion.We reminisced about the time she had a "come-as- you-are" party when we were in twelfth grade. She had been smart enough to warn me about it, but I didn't take the hint, so Saturday morning she came up to my bedroom and dragged me out of bed in my jeans with the butt worn out and an old gray sweatshirt. I still have a picture of me in those jeans. All of her other friends had on lovely pajamas with designs of flowers on them, but the thing I still remember as being so kind is that they all laughed WITH me and said, "Isn't that just like Emily to be different?" I never asked Judy if she had warned them not to laugh AT me. It would have been something she would think of.

Come-as you-are party outfit

I could write a long chapter of how much her friendship meant to me. I was a lonely, skinny, gawky teenager, and Judy and her family made me feel included in theirs.

She ended up having four boys, one of whom died from cancer when he was a teenager. After Phil died, whenever she had a problem she didn't know how to fix she would say, "I will just ask Phil what to do. He's helped me before. He will help me again." What a wonderful faith. Her last child was an absolutely beautiful daughter named Erika.

I am not exactly sure of the cause of Judy's death, but it seems as if the story goes like this. She was living in senior housing, kind of like I am now, and was injured in a home accident, broke her arm and it didn't heal properly.

She died leaving a lot of kids and grandkids. She was reunited with Phil and left me with a photograph of me in torn jeans, two pierced ears, a tiny scar from being burned once making taffy with her and her sister Darlene, and memories of listening to her singing in church choirs and knowing she was in the audience when I was trying to be a Broadway star.

I loved everything about acting except for learning the lines. Trying out for the part you wanted, waiting to see if you got it, going to pick up your very own copy of the script. I wrote my name on the front cover in large letters and on the back cover in smaller print. Then going through all the pages and highlighting your lines and seeing how big your part was. The last thing we got to do before the real work began was just reading through the script for the first time aloud.

Then came all the movements, what doors to go out and come in and when, picking up the right props. The first time I had to learn the directions stage right and stage left, upstage and downstage. Don't EVER have your back to the audience!! Don't mumble. Some of these lessons came in handy even if I wasn't in a play.

I know that because when our class was graduating from eighth grade, I was the class salutatorian. Helen Widman was valedictorian and rightly deserved the honor. I am pretty sure she never cheated by copying someone's algebra answers and then lying about it. I did that and got away with it because Mr. Schmidt couldn't call me a liar when I looked at him with my eyes wide open as I had learned how to lie and said, "No, I don't know why Joan and I both have the same wrong answers."

I had prepared my speech and practiced it and tried to memorize it, but just to be sure I could get through it, I had written it out and took the copy to the podium and started out okay. I lost my place and started to panic. Now here was the problem. My brother Allan had given me a ring he bought when he was in the Hawaiian Islands, and I was wearing it with great pride. It was just a little too big and a little too heavy, so when I started to panic I put my hands behind my back and started to twirl it on my finger over and over. When I realized what I was doing I panicked some more and the ring flew off my hand. Well, it didn't really fly off, but it did fall off. I couldn't find my place, someone had picked up the ring and was trying to hand it to me, then when I figured out what was happening I grabbed it and stuck it in my pocket all the while trying to figure out what I was saying. Then the biggest mistake I made was when I realized I was talking so softly no one could hear me and the crowd was starting to get restless. I knew how to fix that so instead of increasing my volume a little at a time, I pretty much started to shout. Well, the crowd simmered down and I was able to finish my speech. It was ignored by the audience because they hadn't heard me anyway but the kids sitting behind me watching me almost tearing my finger off had plenty to say about it, all except Helen, who might have been feeling my pain.

Here is one more short anecdote that I think is funny, even though apparently I am the only one who thinks so. I have told it to a lot of people over the years, and none of them has ever laughed as hard as I think it deserves.

We were juniors and seniors in high school getting ready to perform a period piece called *Berkeley Square*. We all had these very elaborate costumes with frills, ruffles, waistcoats and garters. We looked adorable, or we would have if we had been thirty years older. We had been given permission to walk downtown in Waterloo to Bishop's Cafeteria to have supper and advertise our play by being seen and wondered at. We had been given money to pay for our meal in advance, so we could maintain our highbrow characters. We were also advised as much as possible to use some of the dialogue from the play, so people would know we were royalty and not riff raff.

We had not practiced doing this and so were pretty much ad libbing what we thought dukes and duchesses and highnesses might sound like as we asked for macaroni and cheese and jello. I suppose because I had seen movies with these kinds of actors, I must have thought I was an expert on how to talk. Plus, one of my character's lines was something like, "Oh, your Royal Highness," but because I was just not in character, I primped my wig and again shouted, "Oh, Mr. Highness, I wouldn't do that."

Bill Doyle, my very favorite friend who was playing His Royal Highness, caught my eye and started to laugh. I tried to stay calm but started to break up. Soon we were all in convulsions. You know what I am talking about if it's ever happened to you. But when we all were able to stop, one of us would say "Oh, Mr. Highness, how kind you are," and we would start all over. I guess the reason no one has ever thought it was funny was "You had to be there."

The closest I ever got to the big time was when I read in the *Hartford Courant* that there were going to be open auditions for walk-on parts for a play opening at The Hartford Stage. This was my big chance. Producers, directors, the stars of the play would all be at the auditions and I would act my little heart out with a scene I had written. This was when I was maybe thirty years old and my ingénue days were long past. I was a housewife from Connecticut who did laundry and shopped for groceries. I was sure that would all be ignored when the casting director realized I had been in several high school plays and was a regular in our local community theater productions. There was also the added benefit of having a very amateur looking sheet of headshots to present. Who else would think of that?

So I showed up at the theater on a Saturday afternoon. Surprisingly there weren't as many people there as I thought there might be. It didn't occur to me then, but I guess in Waterloo there were fewer aspiring actors than I had imagined.

It didn't seem to me as if I had a long time to wait to be called. By the time I got up to the interviewers, I was ready. I told them my name and thanked them for the opportunity to do this. They asked me what I had prepared. I explained I had written a short monologue about the time I left for California when I was not quite nineteen. I asked them to picture the scene. I am standing at the bus stop on 4th Street and Mulberry. I have two suitcases. My destination is Costa Mesa, and I will stay with my friend's family until Nancy and I can find an apartment. My father and sister Shirley are with me making small talk. I am not listening. I begin speaking to myself.

"Why isn't Ma here? I am so angry she wouldn't come to be with me. I'm scared, and I asked her twice to come and see me off. Shirley and Dad are trying to ignore me because I am so close to crying and they don't know what to say to make me feel better. They know they can't. She tried to make me change my mind." "Why don't you stay home and go out with that boy David you like? You have a job. You won't have to check groceries forever. You can go to business school."

"Ma, I can't do that. I have to go; Shirley and Dad are in the car. Please come with me! If I can't get a job I'll be back in two weeks." "No, you won't. Just go and call me when you get there." She is crying and so am I, and I leave her standing there in our kitchen wiping her eyes with her apron. "I have to go now."

As I finish my monologue I am thinking again of that day and how sad and angry I was. The people have been listening carefully with no interruptions. I stop and sniff a little bit, thank them once again and they thank me for coming. "We have your headshot and your phone number." A pause and then they call the next hopeful.

I didn't get a walk on part but it was a wonderful experience being able to say I had actually done it. It was a kind and professional dismissal, and as my husband was driving me home, I told him I was sure I wasn't going to be the next Helen Hayes but was proud of what I had done.

I have also been happy that I was cast in a couple of great plays at Hole in The Wall Community Theater in New Britain. However there wasn't a part for me in *Barefoot in the Park* with the East Hampton Players! However, I WAS a lot jealous when my husband got cast as the delivery man. He did get cast as "Harry Berlin" in the play *Luv* at Hole in the Wall. I suppose there will be more about that in another very short book. But once more I have been diverted from talking about what I remember as a child. I'm not really good at condensing my stories. One thing will remind me of something else and then the tangent has begun; that's not a bad name for a play, right?

CHAPTER 19

A Story About a Long-Time Friend

me–left, Joan–right

I met Joan Hines when she and I were in third grade at Immanuel Lutheran School in Waterloo, Iowa. We both know we have been friends that long, but I have no memories of the third and fourth grade friendship.

The first time I knew she was my friend was in fifth grade when I talked her into changing clothes with me at Debner's Drug Store.

Her mother made all of Joan's clothes and she had an outfit I desperately wanted. I knew I couldn't ask her to give it to me, so I begged her to let me wear it for one day and she could wear something of mine.

She smuggled her turquoise skirt with the high waist and straps fitted over a white blouse out of her house and my contribution to the crime was a red dress: description long-forgotten.

It was going to be a surprise for our classmates to see us in each others' clothes, so we met in Debner's Drug Store bathroom. I'm not sure why we had to keep it a secret, but I remember being really scared we would get caught.

I'm not sure if anyone noticed because fifth graders are pretty self-absorbed, but I was so happy she let me wear that outfit. I don't know if I knew then that she would always be someone whom I could count on no matter what I needed, but she was. Now that's not to say I didn't envy her!! She had blond hair and was always funny and everyone liked her. As we got older, I was so jealous because she had so many boyfriends and boys always noticed her and ignored me! I was a skinny teenage girl with no figure, so that's not surprising.

After we graduated from Immanuel, she went to high school on the "rich" West side of town and I was at East High on the "poor" side of the Cedar River. She had her friends and I had mine, so we had little in common during those years except our friendship.

She loaned me a dress for my junior prom. Her mother made a beautiful skirt and blouse for me in tenth grade. Her parents took me on vacation with them.

Sometimes when I can't fall asleep, I think of the many times I stayed at her house overnight and visited during the summer. I still can picture her house and her room, and I can feel the kindness of her family.

She found me a job where she worked, and because I was a cashier for two years in high school, I was able to have the courage to move to California and know I'd find a job. I met Les there and the rest is history.

She will always be the friend who asked me to be the bridesmaid at her wedding and one of the first people I called when my husband died and she cried with me. We cried together when her first husband George died and when she found love again with Wayne.

There are too many times to write about when she showed many kindnesses to me, so I'll stop here. I hope anyone who reads this has memories of a friend like Joan. Thank you, my "old" friend!

Chapter 20

I Put Things Off and Don't Finish Things I Start

I have never been good at finishing projects. I started a patchwork quilt once and completed one square. The pattern was called "Road to California." I chose the pattern because I moved to California when I was eighteen, which is as good a reason as any, I guess. It was going to be all done by hand: cut out, arranged, stitched, the whole shabang. I bought ALL the material, once again, the batting, the thread, the backing and the needle threader. I had taken lessons at the University of Connecticut Extension Center in Haddam; this was handy because we lived a half a mile from the building. It's a good thing the classes were free because the materials cost a lot. I could have bought a quilt from the Amish for less than the material for the quilt cost. I started that project during the summer of 1975, finished one square in the fall of 1975, and looked at all the supplies sitting in boxes under the bed until I finally donated them to our church's quilters in who knows when. In the meantime, the one lonely completed square moved with us from Haddam to two houses in Wethersfield. By then I was pretty sure I would never finish the dumb thing, so I took it to a picture framer in Hartford. She framed it and when my husband died in 2012, the square and its frame moved to New Jersey. I wonder if it will ever get to California.

There are many more stories like that one. I would have a great idea. I found out it was going to take a long time to finish whatever it was: becoming an actor, getting a college degree (Les got two associate's degrees), or growing tomatoes. I spent twenty dollars one summer on seeds and supplies and harvested six cherry tomatoes before I threw the pots away.

The one I am most disappointed in was I had a great idea for tissue boxes to make them more useful. I called the Scott Tissue company several times and they never returned my calls. I wrote them letters. I explored the process of getting a patent, but it was too complicated so I gave up. I still think it's a good idea, but I have no prototype or sales projections, so I won't qualify for a spot on *Shark Tank*. If you want to hear more about it, call me!!

I also put things off until the last minute and here is my favorite story to prove it. It's also the last one until I get to the point of this section. There is a section in *The Big Book* of Alcoholics Anonymous where the question is "What's the point?" and just before it's read out loud everyone shouts, "What's the point?" This is another example of "I guess you have to be there." By the way, if you think you have a problem with alcohol, maybe you should be there. You are invited…to hear it for yourself.

It was my first day at East High and I must have been scared, but I'm not sure because I knew I looked beautiful. Joan's mother had made a skirt and blouse for me, and my mother had cross-stitched a complicated design on the sleeves and on the hem of the skirt. I had found my way to my second- period biology class and as I walked into the room, the teacher asked me if I was his new assistant! Good grief. Of course, I said no, but I was so flattered. He might have said that to all the rest of the girls who walked in later. But I didn't think of it then.

That first day he assigned most of the work for the first semester and the final assignment that would make the final grade for the year. This was in September and we had until the end of May to finish it. That was forever as far as I was concerned. Come the middle of April, Mr. Herwig started reminding us of our final grade. I figured it was probably time to start working on it, and so I went to Woolworth's and bought three fish bowls and three goldfish. When I got them home, I set up the experiment on our dining room table. I filled one bowl with plain tap water and one fish. The second bowl had salt water in it with one fish, and the third had distilled water in it with the third fish. The distilled water came from the bottle my mother used for her iron.

There were several scenarios of what happened to all those subsequent fish. Some died from the salt water; some died from not getting the water changed on a regular basis, some thrived in the distilled water even if the water looked stagnant. They had all been thrown out the first couple of days after I brought those first fish home but all my results were based on what happened to those first three. I couldn't afford to replace all those fish!

At the beginning of May, it was time to prove my work. I created all the results out of my imagination and typed it up as a mini thesis. That actually took longer than the experiment because I didn't know how to type. Why didn't I ask my mother, who was a graduate of Gates Business College? Incidentally, when my dad was mad at her about something he would tell her, "You think you're such a hotshot 'cause you graduated from college."

It was now the week we had to show our results to the class and be prepared to explain them to the visitors at the Science Fair. That meant one more trip to Woolworth's to get a large white poster board to show the results, attach the thesis, get three new clean fish bowls and three healthy fish to show what the results would have been if the water had been kept clean. I set everything up in the gym along with the rest of the exhibits from the college bound kids. These were about planets and how oxygen worked, the periodic table, another one with the common names of some of the usual elements like NaCL and H20 for salt and water but more complicated, of course.

Mr. Herwig had graded them before the fair opened and when I walked up to mine, I was shocked to see I had gotten an A-. The parents oohed and aahed as they listened to all of us explain our studies. By the time they were halfway through the exhibits, their eyes were glazed over and all they wanted was to get out of there and have some cookies the home ec kids had made and some glasses of apple cider.

It seems to me in a fair world, I should have gotten an A- in creative writing and a part in any play I ever tried out for.

CHAPTER 21

My Backstory

This section should probably have started before the Thanksgiving Story, but I don't really remember anything that happened before that. All of the following is just hearsay and what I THINK must have happened and what it was like. Some of it is created out of my imagination when I look at the little black and white old pictures saved from seventy and eighty years ago. I have my sisters Anita and Shirley to thank for saving all of those time capsules. Anita's husband Frank didn't throw them away after Anita died, and I am so grateful.

I am struck by the sadness of people when they are interviewed after a tornado. "We lost everything, all the family pictures." They are crying about little pieces of paper. I used to think: "Why aren't they worried about what happened to their house or the tree that fell on the barn?" I know why and so do you. A house and a barn can be replaced, but who will know what Great Aunt Mary looked like before she was old and wrinkled? She was a teenager once and she was beautiful, but who would know that without a picture of her standing in front of that old house before it was blown apart.

I am writing this journal or memoir, whatever you want to call it, so my grandchildren will know what I was like at their age. Of course if I am honest they won't care until they are older. Now they want to have friends, get asked to the prom, and worry if they can pass their English test. But there will come a time when they will wonder.

Also to be perfectly correct, I LOVE the picture of me looking down at my new shoes being reflected in a small puddle of melted snow. There was one of me and my father on the day I was confirmed. He is not in his overalls but a beautiful pair of suit pants, a white shirt, and NO railroad cap. We are both smiling–he with a grin looking like a little boy who is dressed up and knowing he's just the cat's meow, and I am just as fancy as I could possibly be, having not disgraced myself by getting Kool Aid on my new clothes. I was so proud to stand next to my father who was looking so fine and knowing for once I was really pretty, not beautiful but pretty. Because this story is all about me, there will be a bunch of pictures with me in them. But my favorite will have to be there even if it's the only one I can afford to include. And because I am not entirely selfish, some of my family members will show up.

Saturday my daughter and youngest granddaughter helped me clean out the three closets in my small apartment. The result of that "adventure" was finding manila envelopes of pictures and newspaper articles I knew I had but hadn't looked at since I moved here nine years ago. The criteria for throwing out or keeping was if it was covered in dust out it went and if it was a memento of some kind it had to be saved until I decided to keep it or not. I had saved all this through every move I had made, so it was still something I wanted.

California, Connecticut, and New Jersey. I was going to count how many times I have moved in my life, but I lost count after seven in California alone. It's not important except in the context of how important these pictures are that I kept them safe all those sixty-two years.

When I realized what lost pictures would mean to me, I stopped wondering why people cried after a disaster. This next part will be like when Ted on *The Mary Tyler Moore Show* started his speech when he won Newsguy of the Year or whatever it was called: "It all began in a little 5000 watt radio station in Fresno, California…." When my mother found out she was pregnant AGAIN, she must have been surprised and very tired at the thought of washing diapers and all the sleepless nights a new baby would bring. I don't think my dad thought too much about it. He probably remembered being tired a lot after the first four, although he couldn't have been too tired one Spring day or evening in May of 1944.

You already know I had two brothers and two sisters, all older than I was. Anita was seventeen, Allan was sixteen, Shirley was twelve and John was nine; my mother was forty-one and my dad was fifty-five when I was born on January 13, 1945. From what I could tell when I was old enough to understand the dynamics of this baby appearance, John and Allan wanted a boy, if they considered it at all. Anita was getting ready to graduate from high school and working part time at the telephone company as a PBX operator. Now I'm showing off because no one reading this probably knows what a PBX operator is or was; a Private Branch Exchange operator directs calls to the right parties within an organization, like in a hospital. Shirley at twelve loved me from the get go. I might have been practice for her because she ended up having five kids that I ended up babysitting when I was old enough. She asked me once if that's why Les and I had only one child because I babysat for her kids, John's kids and Anita's older girls. Allan's kids got left out because they all lived in California. Was I just tired of taking care of kids? I didn't really have an answer, but as time passed we realized we really loved Michele and didn't see any reason to have any more kids. Because this is supposed to be a story to let my grandchildren know about my history, here is what I have been able to piece together from what they told me.

For some reason, I was born at St. Francis Catholic Hospital in Waterloo, Iowa. No one has been able to successfully explain why we were there. All four of my brothers and sisters had been born at Allen Memorial Hospital in Waterloo, the one where almost all Protestant mothers went to have their babies. Because all of the Engleman and Baldwin parents were definitely Lutheran, what was so different about why I happened to show up with all the nuns in their habits instead of just white uniforms and white caps, which would have been more familiar to my forty-one year old mother? I wondered if her age was the reason. She was much older; her pregnancy might have been considered a higher risk, and Catholic prayers were thought to be more powerful. It's possible Dr. Boston was Catholic, but why weren't the rest of the kids born there? He had been, after all, the family doctor forever. As a matter of fact, he took care of me for another eighteen years until I moved to California.

CHAPTER 22

The Neighborhood

As I was sitting here trying to figure out what to write next, I thought of how protected I felt. Of course, I didn't know that at the time but only now do I see that I was lucky to have been a little girl in the 1950s. It was safe. Only three times did I have a feeling of being scared. Once in the community center story and once when I was walking home from school with my friend Ina, which is another non sequitur or maybe not. I just remembered Ina's middle name; it was Mae. I won't include her last name because I don't know if she's still alive and if she is, I don't have her permission to use it. And once when I found out not everyone liked me as much as my family did. Ina and I lived three blocks from each other and went to the same grade school. She lived in an apartment building above a grocery store, and I was interested in how her family fit into just a few rooms. We had a whole house and there was just my father, mother and me. In her family there were two parents, two girls and a grandmother who had to make do in such a small area. Also, they had to walk up a flight of stairs and had neighbors on the same floor.

There are three things I still have in my long-term memory bank about Ina. One: her birthday was 4-4-44. She always bragged about how special that was and I was jealous and two: her mother tried unsuccessfully to get me to stop biting my fingernails. She would rub this awful red liquid on them. It was probably iodine or merthiolate. It tasted terrible. I just looked it up on Google, and it was banned in the 1990s because it was poisonous!

I want to say I washed it off, but the truth is I am pretty sure I licked it off. Her mother would be happy to know I finally stopped biting my fingernails to the "quick" on my thirtieth birthday. Better late than never. And three: she and I were walking home from grade school one afternoon and just as we were approaching the railroad tracks, we saw a woman dressed in black coming toward us. She looked like one of the witches we must have recognized from some Mother Goose story. She said something and Ina and I started to run. I still don't know what she said, but it must have been something a witch would say. We looked at each other and started yelling and didn't stop running and screaming until we got to Ina's apartment building. I don't know what happened after we got upstairs.

I have often wondered what that poor old lady must have thought when she heard us screaming for no reason and her trying to figure out what we were running away from. I kind of hope she didn't realize it was her. The last time I can remember I was afraid of a stranger in the neighborhood was when I was about seven years old. I expect there will be a few "helicopter parents" who will be horrified. I was able to walk to school by myself when I was seven, and it wasn't every day, but this day Shirley wasn't with me. I didn't think of it then, but I suppose my mother had called some of the people on 4th Street to watch out for me. Those were the days when everybody knew all the families who walked downtown. And no one was rich enough to hold anybody's kids for ransom. After all, my parents were old but they weren't MONSTERS!

I must have been in second grade and I was missing my sister's company. I wanted someone to keep me company on that long walk to Immanuel School. It was seven or eight blocks. It was a nice day, the sun was shining and I was happy when I looked up the block and saw a man walking in my direction. "Now I will have someone to talk to," I thought. And so I waited until he got close enough to me to say "Good morning." I never for a minute imagined this man who looked like my father wouldn't be thrilled to talk to a little girl as cute as I was sure I was. There had never been anybody who had ever said anything mean to me or didn't think I was as sweet as my family knew I was. My hair was in braids across the top of my head, and I knew I had on a pretty dress because my mother had said so when she said goodbye. The kids in our family had learned from our parents that we were always expected to be polite and interested in whoever was in our company. And we expected the grownups to be polite and interested in us too.

I began to go into detail about why I was walking to school alone and that I missed my sister Shirley and asked if I could walk with him and we might be friends. When he said "What makes you think I want to be friends with a little kid like you? I don't know you. Didn't your family tell you to not talk to strangers?" I had been taught that when you were asked a question you were supposed to answer, so I said, "No, why would they?" "Don't talk back to me. I don't want to talk to you or walk with you. I want to walk by myself, so leave me alone." I couldn't understand why he was being like that, and I started to cry and walked away. I don't know where he went or what happened to him. I also don't know what I did either, but I must have gotten to school okay; all I know is it was a big surprise when I found out there were mean people to little girls who just wanted to be friends.

As a postscript to that story, it didn't stop me from talking to complete strangers and finding out as much about them as I can in any kind of chance encounter. I have been teased a lot over the years for doing this. The members of my family can find out more about people in five minutes than most members of their own families know. Is it being interested or just being nosey? I know how my New Jersey friends would answer. But if you are a native of Iowa, your answer would be different.

When I have told this story, I have always blamed the man for being mean and scaring me. Now I can see there was probably another "backstory," and it makes the ending more interesting. The reader can make up his or her ending as to why he acted that way. I have had mine for more than seventy years; maybe it's time to make up a new one.

What Waterloo was like then and what it's like now is pretty different. I don't think I appreciated my life there then like I do now. It was just where I lived and everything that happened there revolved around me.

The people who lived there were from so many different places on the economic levels; it was never mentioned, but it was under the surface. The rich people lived on the West Side of the Cedar River and the middle class lived on the East Side. In grade school, it never seemed to matter where we lived and who we were friends with or where our mothers bought our clothes. That started to change when we got to junior high. The cliques had begun to form, and by high school it was pretty clear who would be the cheerleaders, the smart kids, and the troublemakers. I was lucky because I could adapt pretty well. I was in the school plays. English composition was easy and math kept me out of college, hence the cheating in seventh grade. I spent two horrible weeks in tenth grade trying to figure out algebra, staying up until midnight trying to get x to equal y. I never got one right answer in all that time, so I asked to change into bookkeeping, which incidentally helped when I worked as a cashier for many years and in a bank for many more years. One of the gifts of being adaptable and interested was that I could get along with most of the kids in my classes. They were never my friends and I was never invited to their parties, but I could at least talk to them.

I loved to read and at the end of the school year we always got a reading list for the summer. The English teachers gave each of us paper to keep track of what we read. There is not one title I can list now, but I do know I ALWAYS had more books listed than anyone. Rosemond Du Jardin was my favorite author. Her characters were always girls who couldn't get the boyfriends they wanted. Another problem was their parents couldn't afford the prom dresses they wanted, or they didn't like the ones their father liked. It was always fixed when their father got a second job and gave the girl her dress the night of the prom or the father realized his daughter was grown up and could choose her own dress. Her books showed me how to be a teenager and how happy endings were possible.

CHAPTER 23

A 1955 Library

The East Side library was on the corner of East 5th Street and Mulberry Street in Waterloo. The last time Frank took me to see the things I remember about the city, the building was there but I don't know if it was still a library. So because Google is now the world's biggest library, I checked and it's still there, listed on the National Registry of Historic Places. It's no longer a library, but just like everything near and dear to any of us, it's been turned into just another government office building. The good news is it can't be knocked down. I was just looking at the picture of it, and it's not the way I see it in my mind. It's white and I thought it was brown! According to the Google info, the library is a stone building built on a basement; apparently according to the information on the web, this was an unusual architectural feature. Now it's the library I know because the basement is where I found out about books. If a child was under twelve, this was the library in which we were allowed. Also it was not called the young people's library; it was the children's library. Also like some kind of criminal, we had to walk around the corner from the beautiful columned door facing the street and enter by a small wooden door with several steps leading down to the main library rooms.

The first thing I would see was the desk where the librarians kept their magic pencil and their ink pad. It seems as if they were always standing. I don't see a chair when I look at them.

I have no clear picture of how they really looked, only what I can imagine: eyeglasses, hair in a bun, plain, black dresses with a brooch of unknown design at the collar, and black shoes with very low heels. I always knew they would help me find anything I wanted or needed. It never seemed as if any kid was ever bothering them as long as we behaved and kept quiet as we read or worked.

In 1955, there were no computers or cell phones, no displays of new books brought into circulation. The only telephone was on the librarian's desk; it was not connected to the outside world, but there just so the adult section upstairs could get in touch with the downstairs. Every book was on a shelf. There were several cabinets with drawers with labels announcing this was where to find the information about anything that was real. This was the Dewey Decimal System. I have never been able to figure out what the number 641.5 or anything like it meant. (I played it safe on the number and it's got something to do with making cakes. Thank you, Nolan at the Waterloo Public Library for keeping me accurate.) I wasn't sure what you might find if you looked it up. Now if I need to know how to make a cake, there are hundreds of recipes on the internet. There were many more wooden cabinets with drawers in them with small cards labeled A through B, C through D, only one drawer for W, X, Y, and Z, and so on. These were for fiction, which was not a word I used until I was older. I wanted to read about lives different from mine. That is where I would be headed.

I was never really aware of other people being in there with me. It was always quiet and dark. There were, of course, electric lights suspended from the ceiling on long chains but most of the light was from the clerestory windows in the basement.

I was going to try and describe what it looks like and actually do some research on how many shelves and what kinds of books were on each shelf. I wanted to be able to be able to describe what it felt like in this space. I have always pictured it as being kind of holy. It was safe and a little dusty and magical. I would always be wondering what kind of a story I would find. Since I am not a good enough writer to convey the magic, I will ask you to look up the descriptions in *The Human Comedy*, a coming of age story set in California written by William Saroyan and *A Tree Grows In Brooklyn* written by Betty Smith. This is from the viewpoint of a young girl in the early 1900s. They are, after all, the pages where I developed my pictures of the libraries I knew.

CHAPTER 24

My New Writing For March of 2024

If you have ever said, "I could write a book," try it. It's really hard. I want this to be a story for my grandkids, but I also am hoping it might be on the bestseller list of *The New York Times* for fifty weeks straight and win a Pulitzer Prize. I want it to touch somebody's heart in the same way my heart has been touched by some of the wonderful books I've read. But my problem is I've read so many books and articles and stories in my life, been in a few book clubs, and been assigned books to read in ten or twelve classes in schools. I used to have the notion that if I started a book, I was supposed to finish it. Now if I haven't fallen in love with it in fifty pages, I send it back to the library. I feel bad for the author because I realize how hard they worked on it. Some books I have read because I saw the movie and wanted to see if the book was better. It ALMOST ALWAYS is.

I have found that people who like to read and read a lot are most of the time snobby about how much they read and what they read, like it's some great virtue if they know Shakespeare quotations or can talk about the last book club recommendation. I must admit that I have done this; I just read something I really love and then go on and on about it, hoping the person I told about it will read it and love it as much as I did. This actually happened. I couldn't wait to be able to suggest the next book club choice. I wanted everyone to love *A Tree Grows In Brooklyn* as much as I did. I had read it at least five or six times.

Let's just not add salt to the wounds. Not everyone loved it! But then a friend, you know who you are, thinks *Moby Dick* is perfection. I tried to give it a shot because I really wanted to like it for my friend's sake, but I just can't see it. My idea of something that is perfect is *A Child's Christmas in Wales* by Dylan Thomas. Then once when I lived in Wethersfield, I took a writing class and the leader told us to beware of "the little darlings" in our writing, those sentences we think are wonderful but aren't. I love those, so I will have to have an editor or friend cut them out when I turn this over because I won't be able to judge. Once I started a mystery, a "cozy" along the lines of an Agatha Christie story. I have gotten quite a ways into it and I think it's pretty good. My problem is I have lost parts of it–not lost exactly, but some of the pages have been mixed up with other stories. I would like to think I can finish it if I have enough patience to see if I can figure out the order of the pages.

I wrote the following short bit for a writing class I was taking at a community college in Toms River, NJ. When I got it back, the instructor's comment was something along the lines of, "Emily, your story is well-written, but it sounds too preachy. Also, you are telling us how we should feel about our birthdays." I suppose she was right, so you can be the judge after you have read it. Okay? Anyway it's my story. So ha ha!!

After I left Waterloo and moved to California, until she died in 2004 from cancer, my sister Shirley would call me every January 13th and tell me this story: Anita and I were asleep in the front bedroom downstairs. I woke up to the sound of Dad shoveling coal into the furnace. I must have dozed off for a few minutes because the next thing I remember is him opening the curtain and looking at us. He looked tired but was smiling. Anita asked, "Is Ma all right?" "Yes, you have a sister! She and the baby are fine." I was so happy because I really wanted a sister. Anita was wide awake now and not so happy because she had wanted to go back to sleep. She was relieved Ma was ok because she was forty-one, and she knew it was more dangerous to have a baby at that age. "Have you named her yet?" "Yes, but she wants to wait to tell you herself."

Allan shook Dad's hand and when John saw him do that, he realized it was the right thing to do and so he did the same thing. "Let's have a cup of coffee and I can tell you about it."

We weren't able to see you until you came home. Anita and I were sure you were the prettiest baby ever born at St. Francis, and Allan and John pretended not to be interested. So that's how we found out about your birthday.

Shirley always told it the same way every time. She always cried a little when she told me the story because she wanted me to know how happy everyone was that I was there and how much they all loved me.

My idea for birthdays is that we celebrate with as much enthusiasm as possible. Each one of us is an absolutely one of a kind person. We have each been created by God or some combination of cells and miracles so that there never has been or ever will be another just like us.

As I type this tonight on March 12, 2024 there are approximately 8 billion people on the earth, and I don't have any idea how many have gone before us. Every one of all those people have been different, so it seems to me we should take one day a year and remind ourselves what a unique thing we have brought to the world. You don't need to tell anyone what that is, but pat yourself on the back for being you! Have a cake with a candle, call your parents, and say thank you. Shirley always made me feel that way when she called me and told me that story. My hope for all of us is that there will be a moment when we realize the world would not have been the same if we weren't in it, just like George Bailey in *It's a Wonderful Life*. Think of yourself as having run into Clarence when you're reading this!

My husband Les told me once he always felt a little sad when Shirley called me and told me about what happened on my birthday. He had been adopted and didn't have any memories or stories of when he was small. I asked him if he would like me to write one for him about how it might have happened. He said yes, and so I did; it was a mistake though. He knew enough about the circumstances to realize it couldn't have happened that way. When I asked him if it was okay, he said, "It's a nice story, but it isn't true, is it?" I don't know what he did with the book I had written it in. He kept all of his journals and I found a lot of them and read them after he died, but I never found that one.

CHAPTER 25

The Butterfly Effect and How I Met My Husband, Les

In looking at the list of possible stories to include, I realized I was beating myself up about how I had treated some of my friends. It occurred to me that I had actually done all of those things and might include them after all, but not now.

I wasn't really as bad as all that, or maybe I was, but this is a much better story. For some reason my granddaughters are interested, so this is for them. I knew when I moved to California I had a plan to stay there, but I lied to everybody and just said I was going for a visit. I told my boss I was going to stay with my sister-in-law and keep her company when she had her baby because my brother was in the Navy overseas! I was and still am a creative liar. The only true part of that story is that Allan was in the Navy. My plan was to get an apartment with my high school friend Nancy who had moved there to go to beauty school. I would get a job and that was as far as I had planned. I want the word that describes how ambiguous my thoughts were. "Ambiguous" is pretty close, but nebulous is better. *The Oxford Dictionary* defines it best: "unclear, vague, or ill-defined."

I left Waterloo on October 10, 1963 and arrived in Costa Mesa a week later. I traveled by bus and spent an overnight at the YWCA in Salt Lake City. While I was there, I visited the Mormon Tabernacle Temple and saw the movie *Cleopatra*. I have always thought that was a strange combination of things to do.

I want to explain something. I come from Iowa that is flat and green in the summer and flat and brown in the winter. I had been on the Greyhound bus for a few days and seen lots of new things, but when the bus crested the top of the mountain looking down on Salt Lake City with the sun setting behind the range of mountains, it was one of the most beautiful sights I had ever seen. It must have been the same sight the settlers of Salt Lake City saw when they first looked down at that valley and knew they were home.

Anyway, I was at the end of my bus ride and met Nancy; her sister-in-law took me job hunting, and I had a job in less than a week. When the manager of the Thriftimart grocery stores heard I was from Iowa, he said the boss needed to hire me because people from the Midwest were hard workers. Plus, I went directly to "journeyman" cashier immediately and made the top pay for a cashier. I suppose it didn't hurt that I was friendly and knew how to shmooze. Nancy and her sister-in-law found an apartment while I was learning how to work in a great big grocery store. I never did learn all the different kinds of produce grown in California. I had never seen an artichoke or parsley till I became a cashier at Thriftimart. If I didn't know what something was, I made up the price. As I write this, I wonder if maybe the manager took pity on me because I was only nineteen and away from home for the first time.

I will come back to this story after I digress for a while.

Writing this memoir or whatever I'm calling this endeavor continues to be a revelation to me. I had not expected now to realize how brave I was then. I don't know if I was brave or just naive or dumb. I do know I was never afraid to try something. I had a backup plan and a little money. I knew I could find a job. My brother and his family lived close enough that if I needed them they could come from San Diego to Santa Ana to help. I just knew Nancy and I would be fine.

It certainly was a safer time in 1963. The Hillside Strangler, the Night Stalker, and Charlie Manson were not in the news yet. I would work until 10:00 at night and walk home, and not once did anybody ever bother me. In fact, one of the stories I would tell to horrify my friends is this. One night I couldn't sleep so I got dressed and walked to downtown Santa Ana. The way I remember it is I didn't so much walk as I ambled. I got back to the apartment about one o'clock and Nancy was so mad. "Where have you been? I was so worried!! Don't ever do that again!" The reaction is always,

"Don't you know you could have been killed?" "Yes, but I wasn't, was I?" I must admit I never did it again, though.

On my days off, once in a while I would decide to get on one of the city buses and just see where it would take me. My mother came to visit me and we wanted to go to Disneyland. It is in Anaheim, and we had to get there by bus from Santa Ana. I had no idea how to do it, so we just got on the first bus we saw and asked, "How can we get to Disneyland by bus?" The bus drivers kept giving us directions. We kept getting off and on buses till we got there! When I took a day trip to Santa Ana in 2013, I did the same thing: got on a bus and rode around till I got back to the bus terminal. Not one single thing looked familiar. When I got back to the terminal, I asked a cab driver how much he would charge me to go to all the places I wanted to visit: my old apartments, Thriftimart, and the route I had taken on my midnight walk. For $60.00, I found out all three of the apartments had been knocked down and were public parks. The Thriftimart building was still there but empty. The floors still had the image of where the aisles used to be. I could see the outline of the booth where the customers could cash their checks and where we balanced the cashiers' money drawers before they left for the day. Even the length of the produce aisle was still visible. It was kind of sad, but there were some wonderful memories of being so young and carefree when I worked there.

I knew I would be able to get a job in California because I had worked at Clute's Grocery Store in Waterloo as a cashier while I was in high school. I knew I wasn't going to be able to go to college because my math scores were so low, and I knew I would have to work if I wanted graduation pictures and a yearbook and a graduation cap and gown.

Our high school offered credits toward graduation if a student wanted to go to school part time and work part time. There were three choices: trade school, secretarial/office and retail. These were still the days when girls didn't think about learning automotive skills or how to be a plumber or carpenter, so trade school wasn't anything I even considered. For some reason I never took typing, and I still "hunt and peck." My mother attended Gates Secretarial College and one time demonstrated the Gregg Stenography shorthand. I knew I could never do that, so I decided the retail choice was for me. Because I had not been able to figure out algebra when I was a sophomore, I changed to bookkeeping, so I knew debits and credits and how to balance a checkbook. Plus, I got the added benefit of meeting Bill Doyle who was a junior and became one of my best friends.

Bill Doyle, Roland and Les Lourigan remain three of the people I will always cherish because they taught me what was funny and how to laugh.

My best friend Joan worked at Clute's and got me the cashier job, so I could work half days and go to classes the rest of the day. What a blessing it turned out to be, and I have always figured my life turned out the way it did because I knew how to run a cash register. I was really accurate when I made change, and without ANY help from the register I might add!

So things were going along okay. I was earning $3.50 an hour and working 35 hours a week. My share of the rent was $35.00 a month plus my part of the utilities, so I knew I wouldn't need to move back home. My routine was pretty much settled, and I knew I would be able to keep my job. On Friday morning, November 22nd, I was home alone thinking about what time I would have to catch the bus to get to work on time and listening to the radio when I heard the announcer say, "President Kennedy has been shot!" I don't remember what my thoughts were except I started to cry. I wanted to hear my mother's voice and have her tell me everything was going to be alright. I called her with no thought about how much a long distance phone call would cost; I just knew she could help.

I have no idea what she said, but I know she must have prayed with me. I was crying and told her I was scared and didn't know what to do. That is all I remember from that. The next thing that's clear is I knew I had to go to work and get to the bus stop. Several Mexican women were waiting there with me, and no one was talking at all. I couldn't hear any of the usual city noises of car horns and kids yelling. There were probably church bells tolling, but I'm not sure. I worked from 5:00pm to 9:00pm. The customers, the few who were there, were silent and looked shocked and confused. I know I started to cry again if I saw a woman trying not to cry. I walked home, still not understanding what I should do. I went to bed and slept. On Saturday, I was scheduled to work eight hours and nothing was clear to me except to make sure my cash drawer was right at the end of the day. On Sunday, Nancy and I went to church and found out the man who killed the president had been shot too.

Somehow we must have gotten a hold of a television because we watched the funeral proceedings with the riderless horse and young John saluting the casket. The eternal flame was lit and now JFK is just a memory to millions of people–and to many just a name in a song with Martin Luther King and Bobby Kennedy. It had not occurred to me then or until now when I looked it up that Thanksgiving was so close to the assassination.

The reason this date is important is this: the stars were aligned. Nancy's boyfriend was stationed on the USS *Canberra* in San Diego and called her to come down and see him on the ship over Thanksgiving. Santa Ana and San Diego are only ninety miles apart, and she could take the bus. If I went along, I could call my sister-in-law Rose who lived on Point Loma and we could stay with her. I had only worked at Thriftimart for a little over a month, but when I asked my boss for the weekend off and explained my brother's wife needed me to babysit for my niece and nephew in San Diego, the final detail was in place when he said yes. We did in fact stay with Rose and her kids, but we did not do any babysitting. A lot of the butterfly effect is because I was and still am a really spontaneous liar. If Rose had needed a babysitter, she had a family of sisters and a mother who would have stepped in.

So Bob and his friend Les met us at the bus station in San Diego and the rest is history. Bob broke up with Nancy sometime later; she married a policeman I think and is still married to him as far as I know. Les and I were married six months later and stayed married for almost fifty years. I started out telling you why I went to California and then went to how I met Les. I suppose in some way they are connected. If I hadn't gone to California I would never have met him, but if I hadn't worked at Clute's I would never have gone to California.

It seems as if I always knew at some level I would need to leave home and see the world. I thought it would be to go to New York City with Judy, but she got married and I wasn't brave enough to go by myself, so I chose the next "escape," which is really the only word I can think of to describe it.

An escape was not consciously on my mind if I am honest. I was dating this guy who worked in the produce department–this is the first time vegetables and fruit made a difference in my life. It was probably inevitable that I didn't marry him because he had a name I thought was too "country." I was pretty sure I wouldn't be able to be romantic for the rest of my life with somebody named Orville, but I dated him pretty seriously for a few months. He had a nice car and he was smart enough and just a little bit older than I was, so he kind of knew his way around. He could buy beer and we went to parties with the older people at the store. He had met my mother and father and had visited my house a few times. I think I was beginning to think it might get serious, and I was okay with that.

One afternoon in probably August because it was really warm, he drove me home from a Sunday ride and parked in front of my house. I had no idea that what he was going to say would change who I was and what I wanted from life. He told me he was going to have to break up with me because he wanted to get married, and I wouldn't be the kind of wife he needed or wanted. I had no idea what he was talking about until he started to explain. He wanted a house with a picket fence and a wife who kept the house clean. He saw how my mother kept house and knew I would be the same. He wanted order and a wife who would be happy with coffee hours with women friends, who went to PTA meetings and was quiet and wouldn't try to boss him around like my mother did my dad.

Looking back on it, I wish I had stormed out of the car, slammed the door, and told him what I thought of him, but I didn't. I started to cry and told him I could change. I was heartbroken, but he said he had made up his mind. I got out of the car very quietly and went into my house with the unmatched wallpaper and the parents who were doing their best to keep me happy, and I was ashamed that he was right. And then I was ashamed that I was ashamed. I couldn't explain why I was crying, but I asked if I could borrow the car and go see my friend Joan. I knew she would help. I talked. She listened. I felt better. When I got home and started to think about it, I realized I didn't want all the things Orville wanted. If I couldn't go to New York, I could go to California and see the ocean and mountains. I could earn my own money and spend it the way I wanted to. I didn't have to settle for kids and a house and bills. I could do whatever I wanted and be whoever I wanted. Mrs. Goodhousekeeping didn't have to be me.

That anger and sadness and joy happened in an afternoon and night in August of 1963, and on October 10, 1963, I left for a different life. I had no idea what was in store, but I was excited to find out. Shirley was happy I was leaving home; as I got on the bus to leave she scolded me, "Have fun and don't get married right away." My mother cried because she didn't want me to leave. She was afraid for me maybe, or maybe she didn't want to be left alone with just my dad and would miss me.

CHAPTER 26

A Few Final Thoughts

I will mention some of the things I have done these last few days. They might give you an idea how I have spent my life more or less recently.

I finished a really good book called *The Watch That Ends the Night* by Allan Wolf. I found it in our library in our building. I am not going to go into the details except to tell you it's about some of the real passengers and crew of the Titanic.

Today is Thursday April 18th and I will start with Sunday April 14th. That's easy; it's my daughter's birthday. I went to church after spending twenty minutes trying to decide what to wear. The skirt I wanted to wear was too big, so I tried to move the waistband button over, but I couldn't figure out how to thread the needle. So I gave up and wore the skirt anyway. Before you judge me, do YOU know how to use one of those stupid needle threaders?

I sang an Easter anthem in the choir and visited with my friend who told me to get busy with my story. Don't ever ask her to hold you accountable if you don't mean it. She's tough! I took my daughter and granddaughter to dinner at a German restaurant. It was Michele's birthday. The weird part of it was that some weeks before, I had told her I wanted to take her out for her birthday and then told her where I wanted to go. She thought that was strange, but she wanted to humor me because I haven't been the same since my back surgery. I blame it on the aftereffects of the anesthetic, but I don't know how long I can use that as an excuse. She and Sarah went along with it and convinced me that's where they wanted to go, too. They seemed to enjoy the food, but I was disappointed because my mother cooked her version of goulash once a week when I was growing up, and this was nothing like it. The restaurant version was spicy and had all kinds of vegetables and seasoning and broth. My mother made hers with hamburger, tomato juice and elbow macaroni, and I loved it. Again, don't judge me. That's what we could afford. I still don't know how to cook with spices.

When Les and I were first married, I made lunch for him when he worked as a corpsman on Treasure Island. He came home after a few days of eating my lunches and asked me as nicely as he could, "Emily, could you please put more than one slice of lunch meat on my sandwiches? The guys are giving me grief!" I thought that's how you did it! That's how we did it at home.

So anyway, we had a good time at the birthday party after I got the dessert and some of the best coffee I ever had. I came home and played poker with some of the people in our building and lost maybe a dollar and a half.

For those of you who know what this means, you are going to be astonished at what happened. We all were. If you don't know what it means, just know it doesn't happen very often. We had decided it was going to be the last hand because it was time for supper. We were playing five card draw, jacks or better to open. I was dealt a royal straight flush, ace high in hearts. A perfect hand! I will leave it to you to figure out the razzing I got from the guys from North Jersey I was playing with!

I am including this list for my own satisfaction so I can share some books that I have enjoyed and have been important to me. It's kind of like a commercial. It's not really important watching them but maybe something that might be useful to know that you won't need to ask your doctor to prescribe!

A list of ten of my favorite books:

1. *A Tree Grows in Brooklyn* by Betty Smith
2. *Little Women* by Louisa May Alcott
3. *To Kill a Mockingbird* by Harper Lee
4. *The Nightingale* by Kristin Hannah
5. *The Murder of Roger Ackroyd* by Agatha Christie
6. *Knots and Crosses* by Ian Rankin
7. *Centennial* by James Michener
8. *East of Eden* by John Steinbeck
9. *The Girl With the Dragon Tattoo* by Stieg Larsson
10. *Jane Eyre* by Charlotte Bronte

PGIL2024USA